Lucifer

BOOK FOUR

Mike Carey
Writer

Peter Gross
Ryan Kelly
P. Craig Russell
Marc Hempel
Ronald Wimberly
Artists

Daniel Vozzo
Lovern Kindzierski
Colorists

Jared K. Fletcher
Letterer

Christopher Moeller
Cover Art

Christopher Moeller
Michael Wm. Kaluta
Original Series Covers

Based on characters created by Neil Gaiman,
Sam Kieth and Mike Dringenberg.

LUCIFER BOOK FOUR

DC Comics, 2900 W. Alameda Avenue, Burbank, CA 91505
Printed in the USA. Second Printing.
ISBN: 978-1-4012-4605-1

Library of Congress Cataloging-in-Publication Data

Carey, Mike, 1959- author.
Lucifer Book Four / Mike Carey, Peter Gross.
pages cm
Summary: "Cast out of Heaven, thrown down to rule in Hell, Lucifer Morningstar has resigned his post and abandoned his kingdom for the mortal city of Los Angles. Emerging from the pages of writer Neil Gaiman's award-winning series The Sandman, the former Lord of Hell is now enjoying a quiet retirement as the proprietor of Lux, L.A.'s most elite piano bar. A deadly new threat to all of Creation emerges and battles lines are drawn. As forces in Hell and on Earth prepare for a final struggle for supremacy, we venture across time and space and even places in between to follow the path of the players in the battle to come." — Provided by publisher.
ISBN 978-1-4012-4605-1 (paperback)
1. Graphic novels. I. Gross, Peter, 1958- illustrator. II. Title.
PN6728.L79C44 2014
741.5'973—dc23
2014011711

MIX
Paper from responsible sources
FSC® C101537

Table of Contents

INTRODUCTION

For a guy who never worked on Neil Gaiman's THE SANDMAN, I've spent a lot of time working in the sandbox that Neil created for it — maybe more than any other artist working in comics. For starters, I was the primary artist on the ongoing THE BOOKS OF MAGIC series, featuring Neil's pre-Harry Potter boy wizard, Timothy Hunter (I even wrote the title for its last two years). After that, I fell into LUCIFER, a soon-to-be-epic story based on Neil's fabulous version of the Fallen One from the pages of THE SANDMAN that was written by a (then) relatively unknown writer named Mike Carey. I'm not sure why I gravitate to this sort of material, or why it gravitates to me, but I can hazard a guess or two:

1) I like big complicated stories that are about something that feels meaningful.

2) I like it when the story makes you question and consider things in a new light, and demands that you pay attention.

You can't find those sorts of stories very often in superhero comics, but you can find them more often than not at Vertigo, and you can always find them in LUCIFER. That's why I like working with Mike Carey, and why I continue working with him on our current ongoing series THE UNWRITTEN; he likes the same sort of stories as I do, and he's so damned good at writing them. They're stories with meat on their bones. They have substance, and you might find yourself thinking about them long after you're done reading them.

When I looked over the issues collected in this volume (having worked on them, I've probably never been able to experience them as a normal reader does), I was instantly struck by how well they are written, how many great lines there are, and how many great character moments. I don't think anyone in comics writes better dialogue than Mike, and he does it without being flamboyant or insistently demanding your attention. He does it by following the easier-said-than-done rule that characters in stories should say things that are more interesting than what we hear in everyday life.

But since this is the fourth volume of the collected LUCIFER that you're reading, chances are that you already know all this. So instead of belaboring my point, I'll tell you something that you may *not* know

(I certainly didn't until I started writing this intro): Mike and I are one of the all-time greatest writer/artist teams in comic book history — or at least among the most prolific. Together, we have created well over 125 full-length comic books. When I realized this, I thought that that had to be close to the top issue count for a writer/artist team at Vertigo, but after looking into it I discovered that cracking the 100-issue barrier is a rare feat in *all* of comics — and that those who have done it are some pretty special combos: Stan Lee and Jack Kirby, Garth Ennis and Steve Dillon, Robert Kirkman and Charlie Adlard, Brian Azzarello and Eduardo Risso, Bill Willingham and Mark Buckingham. And when I put the question out on Facebook, I got Marv Wolfman and Gene Colan, Marv Wolfman and George Pérez, Brian Bendis and Mark Bagley, Mark Evanier and Sergio Aragonés. There are more, and I can pretty much guarantee they're all comic book gold. That's because you have to build something pretty special to do that many issues together.

Mike and I clicked from the first issue we did together, and we continue to click thousands of pages later. But there are things that change along the way when you become two sides of the same storytelling coin. You each understand what the other is after, and you know how to get there. Mike knows that I might completely ignore the staging that he includes in his scripts, but he also knows that his staging may be the thing that acts as a springboard to take me to a better place. I love surprising a writer with something that he didn't ask for which turns out to be exactly what he wanted. I imagine that it must be frustrating sometimes to write stories that someone else draws — to get invested in a picture in your mind and then see it realized in quite a different way. But I think that what Mike and I succeeded at in LUCIFER and THE UNWRITTEN is keeping each other surprised and engaged in the story. We might have a long conversation about an upcoming issue, but when the script arrives it's always full of new things that we never talked about — things that came to Mike as he spent more time with the story. This allows me to see it fresh again, and when I draw it I usually come up with an interpretation that Mike didn't expect. It's those moments that take the story down unexpected paths. I think that's the secret of a good collaboration — you have to create something greater than the parts.

This is starting to read disturbingly like a love letter, but it *is* a pretty intimate thing, the relationship between comics writer and artist, especially when it lasts beyond that magical 100-issue milestone.

This volume is a result of that sort of team-up. This is Mike and I (and all of our gifted cohorts) hitting our prime and firing on all cylinders. And whether you're reading it for the first time or the umpteenth time, you're in for a treat.

To finish, I'll share a little epiphany I had about the first story in this collection. Mike has often expressed that "Stitchglass Slide" is one of his favorite LUCIFER arcs, and Thole, the stitchglass weaver, is one of his favorite characters. Only as I was writing this introduction did I realize why: the gentle, humble Thole, a loyal weaver of stitchglass, is none other than Mike himself. He weaves love and trust and fear and every other emotion together to form his creations. And he makes those creations not only to express himself, but also to keep his family safe and secure. What could be more like the writer himself? So keep that in mind as you read. As for Thole's female counterpart, I can say with certainty that she doesn't seem at all like Mike's wife, Lin. But if Mike is the creature laboring away on his beloved art, then who could that demanding, bossy, and frightening female represent? Let's just hope it's editors in general, and not anyone specific.

Bringing this back around to the beginning, I've often thought that I owe my house to Neil Gaiman, but I owe everything in it to Mike Carey (and Shelly Bond, for realizing that the two of us would make a good team). I certainly didn't expect that I'd end up working with Mike for as long as I have. But with some luck, maybe we'll make another 100 issues of comics together, and when I write another intro for another one of our collections I'll get to thank Mike for a new house!

It's a funny thing making a living from stories, but I can't think of a better way to dedicate my time. And I'm grateful for every bit of it.

— Peter Gross
Minneapolis, 2014

GRIEF. GRIEF IS JAGGED EDGE GREEN STIPPLE SHOWING THROUGH BLEACHED WHITE. ANGER IS TURQUOISE SHOT WITH RED.
PAIN IS BURNED BLACK.
BURNED BLACK. THE GODS SHOUTING THUNDER THROUGH THE SKY.
OVER MY SMASHED HOUSE WHERE THE BOY LIE BLEEDING.
THE DANGER WAS MINE. THE DANGER WAS MINE THAT I BRINGED HIM INTO.
BUT I TRIED THEN TO HELP THE BOY. WITH MY OWN LIFE TRIED I TO SAVE THE BOY.
BURNED BLACK. FOR THE EMPTY EGGS WERE MY FUTURE AND HER FUTURE, TOO.
AND IN ALL THE WORLD NOW, NOTHING DOES BE TO FILL THEM.
LISTEN.
I WILL TELL YOU THE COLORS OF IT.

AND I *BUILDED* THERE. OH YES.

SENDED OUT MY WEB ALL EVERYWHERE, TO *TOUCH* WHERE PEOPLE FEEL. TOUCH IT AND *TAKE* IT.

WEAVED THE FEELINGS INTO STITCHGLASS. *JOY* FOR THE EGG CHAMBER. HUNGER FOR THE FEEDING PIT.

LOVE, LOVE, LOVE FOR THE TOWER TIP TOP, FOR THE *BAIT.*

I AM *THOLE,* WHO SPINS IN EVERY COLOR!

I AM THOLE, KING OF *STITCHGLASS,* KING OF *LOVE!*

TWO *RINGS* I MAKED TO KEEP THE HOUSE SAFE. THE FIRST DID BE OF FORGETFULNESS, SO THE HOUSE WOULD SLIDE OUT OF THE *MINDS* OF EGG STEALERS.

BUT FOR THE INNER RING I NEEDED *FEAR.*

RABBITS FEAR FOXES. BIRDS FEAR CATS. MEN FEAR *EVERYTHING.*
WEB IS *FULL* OF FEAR, BUT I DID LOOK FURTHER, FURTHER.
THEN FINDED I THE *FOUNTAINHEAD.*
THEN FINDED I THE *MAKER.*
STITCHGLASS SLIDE I
The Weaving
MIKE CAREY-WRITER
PETER GROSS & RYAN KELLY
ARTISTS
JARED FLETCHER-LETTERING
DANIEL VOZZO-COLORS AND SEPARATIONS
CHRISTOPHER MOELLER-COVER PAINTER
MARIAH HUEHNER-ASSISTANT EDITOR
SHELLY BOND-EDITOR
BASED ON CHARACTERS CREATED BY
GAIMAN, KIETH AND DRINGENBERG

THIS ISN'T VERY PRIVATE, LUCIFER.
I HAD MY DOUBTS, ELAINE BELLOC, BUT YOU SEEM TO HAVE ADAPTED FAIRLY WELL TO THIS ROLE.
THAT'S WHY I'VE COME TO YOU NOW-- INSTEAD OF JUST DOING WHAT NEEDS TO BE DONE.
PRIVACY IS FOR THOSE WHO'VE GOT SOMETHING TO HIDE.
THANKS, I GUESS.
BUT--
--DOING WHAT, EXACTLY?
WHAT IS THIS ABOUT?
IT'S ABOUT ADAPTING TO A NEW SITUATION.

YOU MEAN GOD GOING AWAY, OR THE *TITANS* STORMING HEAVEN?
YOU'VE BEEN KEEPING UP WITH CURRENT *EVENTS*. GOOD.
I MEAN *BOTH.*

I'M AWARE THAT THERE ARE *IMMORTALS*-- GODS, DEMONS AND THE LIKE-- LIVING HERE IN MY CREATION.
I TOLERATED THIS BECAUSE IT DIDN'T *MATTER* TO ME. NOW IT DOES. I WANT THEM GONE.

GONE *DEAD*, OR JUST GONE *GONE?*
IF I HANDLE IT *MYSELF*, I'LL DO WHATEVER'S QUICKEST.
BUT I'M PREPARED TO ENTERTAIN *ANOTHER* OPTION.

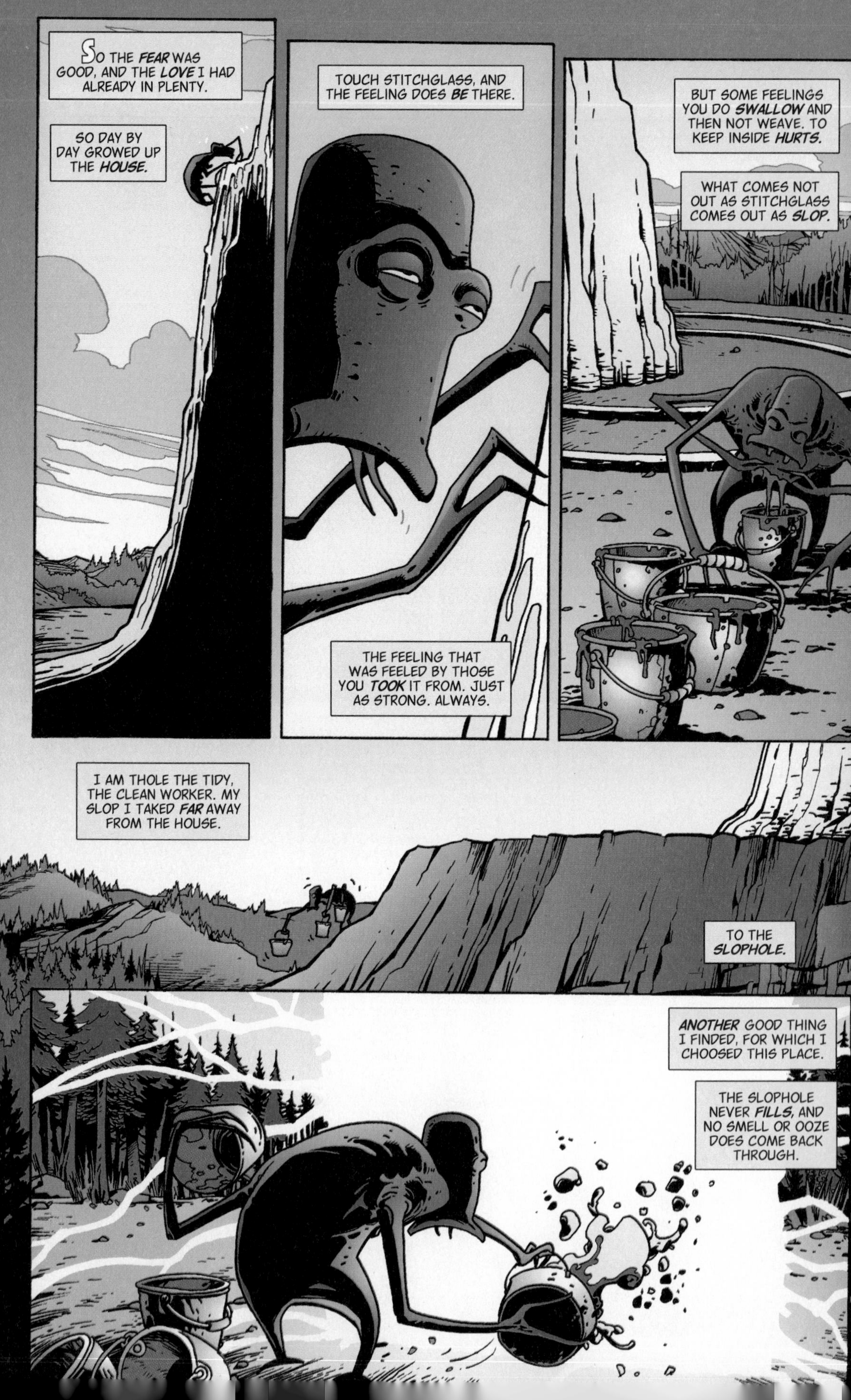
SO THE FEAR WAS GOOD, AND THE LOVE I HAD ALREADY IN PLENTY.
SO DAY BY DAY GROWED UP THE HOUSE.
TOUCH STITCHGLASS, AND THE FEELING DOES BE THERE.
THE FEELING THAT WAS FEELED BY THOSE YOU TOOK IT FROM. JUST AS STRONG. ALWAYS.
BUT SOME FEELINGS YOU DO SWALLOW AND THEN NOT WEAVE. TO KEEP INSIDE HURTS.
WHAT COMES NOT OUT AS STITCHGLASS COMES OUT AS SLOP.
I AM THOLE THE TIDY, THE CLEAN WORKER. MY SLOP I TAKED FAR AWAY FROM THE HOUSE.
TO THE SLOPHOLE.
ANOTHER GOOD THING I FINDED, FOR WHICH I CHOOSED THIS PLACE.
THE SLOPHOLE NEVER FILLS, AND NO SMELL OR OOZE DOES COME BACK THROUGH.

NO OFFENSE.
MARTIN?
NO HURT.
MARTIN, I CALLED YOU FIVE MINUTES--
OH JESUS! WHAT DID YOU DO NOW?
I WAS SCARED OF MY TEDDY AND SO I KILLED HIM WITH THE SCISSORS BUT THEN HE LOOKED SO FUNNY WITH HIS HEAD OFF I JUST LAUGHED AND LAUGHED AND LAUGHED!
MARTIN!
I COULDN'T I COULDN'T I
COULDN'T STOP I COULDN'T--
MARTIN, LISTEN TO ME!
I SAID NO SCISSORS! HOW MANY--?
HOW MANY FUCKING TIMES DID I SAY--?
JUST-- JUST STAY THERE.
I'M GOING TO SEND YOUR FATHER UP TO DEAL WITH YOU.

YOU SAID WHAT? ARE WE PLAYING THAT KIND OF GAME, NOW?

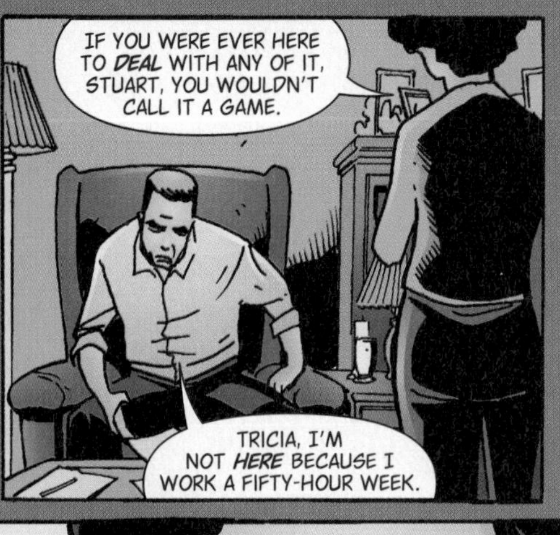
IF YOU WERE EVER HERE TO DEAL WITH ANY OF IT, STUART, YOU WOULDN'T CALL IT A GAME.
TRICIA, I'M NOT HERE BECAUSE I WORK A FIFTY-HOUR WEEK.

IT'S NOT AS THOUGH I--

DON'T YOU DARE THROW YOUR FUCKING JOB IN MY FACE!
I HAD A JOB ONCE, TOO. THAT DISASTER AREA UPSTAIRS WAS YOUR IDEA.
"IT'LL CHANGE OUR LIVES, SWEETHEART." WELL I DON'T SEE WHERE IT'S CHANGED YOURS!

JESUS, HOW CAN YOU EXPECT MARTIN TO BE EMOTIONALLY STABLE? LOOK AT THE EXAMPLE YOU SET HIM!
AT LEAST I'M HERE ENOUGH OF THE TIME TO BE AN EXAMPLE, YOU SELF-RIGHTEOUS BASTARD.

HE WAS SENT HOME FROM SCHOOL AGAIN. FOR HITTING THE TEACHER.
I THINK MAYBE WE SHOULD CALL IN THAT ROUSSEAU GUY. THE ONE YOUR COUSIN RAVED ABOUT.

OKAY.
BUT TONIGHT HE SLEEPS IN THE ATTIC.

NO! I DON'T *WANT* TO GO UP THERE!

IF YOU CAN'T *CONTROL* YOURSELF AROUND OTHER PEOPLE--

--YOU CAN'T *BE* AROUND OTHER PEOPLE.

RATCH

TCHIK

AHUH! AHUH! AHUH!

AAAAAAAAAA!

NOISE. WHERE FROM COMED THE NOISE? SHARP BROWN WITH MISERY, TOO JAGGED TO WEAVE.
THE WORLD INSIDE THE SLOPHOLE IS SMALL AND DARK.
THUD
WHUMP
CRUMP
AND ITS HILLS MOVE UNDER YOUR FEET.
YEAARRRGH!
AAH! AAH! AAH!
OW! OW! OW!
THE ANIMAL'S FEAR WAS TOO MUCH. IT DID MAKE ME BLIND AND DEAF AND HURTING LIKE DEATH.

T WAS HARD TO WEAVE
TRANDS THAT HAD NOT
THAT FEAR IN THEM.
BUT I DID LET IT RUN OVER ME AND THROUGH ME, AND THROWED OTHER COLORS BACK.
PEACE. TRUST. CALM. SLEEP.
I SAW THEN I HAD MAKED A BAD THING HAPPEN. THIS ANIMAL DID LIVE INSIDE MY SLOPHOLE.
THIS ANIMAL DID ABSORB THE BAD-FEELING SLOP AND BE SICK.
SICK WITH BAD FEELING. WITH HATE-LOVE-HAPPY-ANGRY-SADNESS NOT HIS OWN.
NOBODY BUT I COULD FIX. I DID WEAVE A SELF-STONE.
I DID SMILE TO THINK OF AN ANIMAL WITH A SELF. BUT STILL--
--I LEFT IT SLEEPING. FEELING ONLY SELF-FEELINGS.
AT PEACE.
GET UP, MARTIN.
MNUH! DAD, I HAD THIS REALLY WEIRD--
COME DOWNSTAIRS. WE'RE WAITING FOR YOU.

SO THIS IS LITTLE MARKY.
MARTIN.
MARTIN. COME ON OVER HERE, SON.

MY NAME'S ROUSSEAU. YOUR FOLKS HAVE ASKED ME TO HELP YOU.
DON'T NEED NO HELP.
EVERYONE NEEDS HELP, SON. WE JUST DON'T ALL KNOW IT.

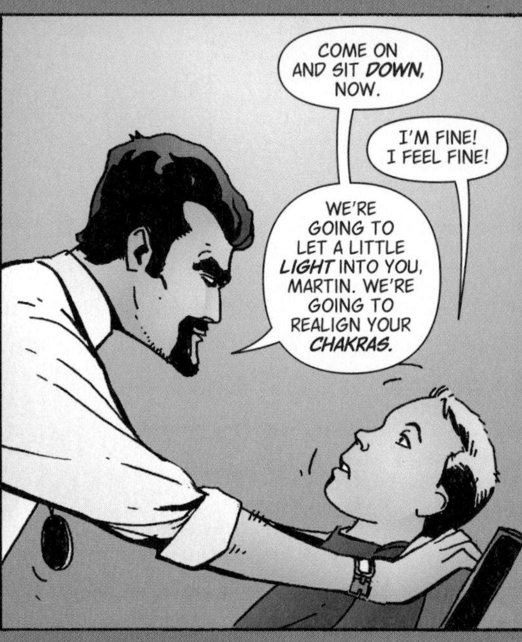
COME ON AND SIT DOWN, NOW.
I'M FINE! I FEEL FINE!
WE'RE GOING TO LET A LITTLE LIGHT INTO YOU, MARTIN. WE'RE GOING TO REALIGN YOUR CHAKRAS.

THIS ISN'T LIKE AN EXORCISM, IS IT, MISTER ROUSSEAU?
LORD NO, MRS. PATERSON. THIS IS SPIRITUAL SCIENCE, NOT SUPERSTITION.
THERE ARE NO DEVILS INSIDE MARTIN.

JUST THE FILAMENTS OF HIS OWN SOUL, CROSS-CONNECTED AND SHORTING OUT.

I'M THE ELECTRICIAN OF THE SPIRIT.

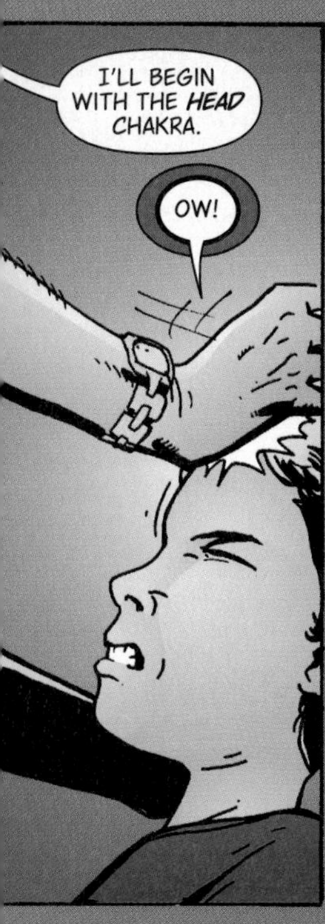
I'LL BEGIN WITH THE *HEAD* CHAKRA.
OW!

CHANT THE MANTRA I TAUGHT YOU, PLEASE-- OR *INTONE* IT INSIDE YOUR HEADS.
STOP IT! THAT *HURTS!*

IT'S THE PAIN OF *REALIGNMENT,* MARTIN. OF EVERYTHING COMING RIGHT AGAIN INSIDE YOU.
IT'LL GET *WORSE* BEFORE IT GETS BETTER.

OOOLF!

MARTIN!
COME *BACK* HERE!

THERE'S NO WAY YOU'RE GETTING *OUT* OF THIS, YOUNG MAN!
THERE'S NOWHERE YOU CAN *RUN!*

I FINISHED MY HOUSE.
MY HOUSE LIKE VOICES SINGING "COME, COME COME!"
BUT NO FEMALES DID LISTEN.
PERHAPS--
--I DID NEED MORE LOVE.
LOVE IS HARDEST TO WEAVE. MANY STRANDS. MANY COLORS ALL MIXED IN.
DEVOTION, TRUST, LUST, POSSESSIVENESS NEED TENDERNESS. SPINNER MUST FIND ALL.
I DID CAST HIGH AND FAR.
UNTIL MY WEB DID STRETCH BETWEEN A MILLION MINDS.
AND IN SOME OF THEM--
--I FINDED WHEREWITH TO WEAVE.

IF IT WERE YOU WHO WERE ASKING--
SHE IS CARRYING OUT MY WISHES, MAZIKEEN.
I WANT THE IMMORTALS GONE FROM HERE. THEY'RE INCONVENIENT.
STILL, IT GOES HARD WITH ME TO BE COMMANDED BY A CHILD.
AND TO SERVE WITH THE LIKES OF THOSE.
YOU THINK SHE'S TALKING ABOUT US?
MUST BE. HER FACE IS SCREWED UP IN DISGUST.
WELL, THE HALF I CAN SEE IS.
ELAINE BELLOC IS A CHILD NO LONGER. SHE HAS GROWN INTO SOMETHING ELSE.
I WANT YOU TO GIVE HER YOUR LOYALTY-- AND TO WATCH HOW SHE WORKS.
THEN I OBEY, MY LORD.
IN THIS, AS IN ALL THINGS.

EXCELLENT FEELINGS! FEMALES WOULD COME FROM EVERYWHERE.
FEMALES WOULD FIGHT EACH OTHER TO MATE WITH ME, FOR MY HOUSE WAS PERFECT, PERFECT--
!
!!!
!!!!!
THE ANIMAL. THE ANIMAL HAD COME OUT OF THE SLOPHOLE.
HOW HORRIBLE! HOW INOPPORTUNE!
YOU! YOU CANNOT STAY HERE, ANIMAL! THIS IS NOT YOUR HOUSE!
WHAT?
GO NOW. GO!
WHY MY CIRCLE DID NOT STOP YOU? MAKE YOU FORGET, OR BE AFRAID TO COME?
HEY! DON'T GO POKING AT ME!
I JUST WANTED TO SEE WHAT YOU WERE DOING.
THE SELF-STONE! IT PROTECTS FROM NOT-SELF FEELING!
YOU WALKED THROUGH MY RINGS AND FEELED NOTHING!

YOU HAVE TO GO HOME, ANIMAL. HOME TO YOUR SLOPHOLE.
I WON'T.
I HATE IT THERE.

I AM DEMON. I WILL EAT YOU AND KILL YOU AND BITE YOU MANY TIMES.
I DON'T BELIEVE YOU.
I'M STAYING.

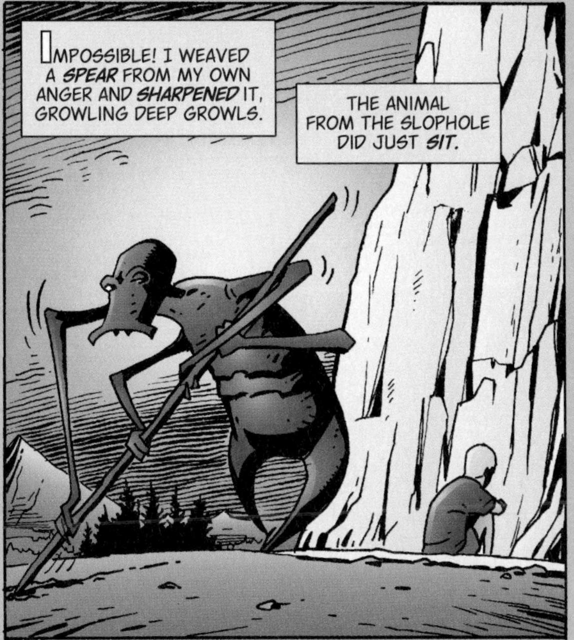
IMPOSSIBLE! I WEAVED A SPEAR FROM MY OWN ANGER AND SHARPENED IT, GROWLING DEEP GROWLS.
THE ANIMAL FROM THE SLOPHOLE DID JUST SIT.

I BUILDED HIGH UP ON THE ROOF FOR MANY HOURS, PRETENDING I WAS ALONE.
THE ANIMAL FROM THE SLOPHOLE DID JUST SIT.

BUT AT EVENING, WHEN THE SUN BOWED TO THE MAKER--
--THE ANIMAL DID BOW ITS HEAD TOO. POURED OUT SADNESS, SADNESS, SADNESS.

ANIMAL, THIS IS NOT GOOD.
YOUR JAGGED BROWN SORROW WILL SCARE AWAY FEMALES.
'M NOT AN ANIMAL! I'M A BOY. MY NAME'S MARTIN.
I CAN'T STOP BEING SAD. OR ANGRY OR SCARED OR LAUGHING WHEN THERE'S NOTHING FUNNY!
THAT'S WHY MY MUM AND DAD SHOUT ALL THE TIME AND HATE ME!
MY DISMAY WAS GREAT THEN. GREAT MY SHAME.
THE ANIMAL-THAT-SAID-IT-WASN'T-AN-ANIMAL WAS HURTING, AND I HAD MAKED THE HURT.
I SENDED OUT MYSELF INTO THE ANIMAL'S SELF.
BEHIND JAGGED BROWN WERE OTHER COLORS.
PALE THEY WERE, AND BRITTLE-OLD.
FOR MOST SPINNERS, TOO WEAK TO WEAVE.
BUT I AM THOLE!
KING OF STITCHGLASS!

WHAT IS THAT THING?
IT IS A SLIDE. OF STITCHGLASS.
SLIDE ON IT, ANIMAL.
BUT IT'S LAME.
IT IS NOT LAME. I DID SPIN IT FROM EXCITEMENT AND JOY.
TRY. SEE.
THAT WAS INCREDIBLE!
NO MORE JAGGED BROWN.
THAT IS GOOD.

WHAT TROUBLE WAS IT? NOT MUCH.
TO WEAVE AN EXTRA ROOM, A LESS THAN ONE DAY'S WORK. TO FEED--
--BOY MARTIN COULD NOT EAT GRASS. SO I COLLECTED THE EARTH-FRUITS AND THE TREE-FRUITS.
NEVER HAD HE FEASTED SO WELL!
HIS MIND, TOO, I FEEDED. TAUGHT HIM THE COLORS OF STITCHGLASS AND THE WAY OF THE SPINNER.
HE DID BE CLEVER AND QUICK TO UNDERSTAND.
IN MOST AREAS.
YOU CAN'T LAY EGGS. THE LADY LAYS THE EGGS.
THE MALE DOES WEAVE THE SHELL, BOY MARTIN.
THE FEMALE FILLS THE SHELL WITH CHILD ESSENCE.
THEN THE MALE--
--THE MALE DOES--
PERHAPS I WILL EXPLAIN THIS THING TO YOU WHEN YOU ARE OLDER.

WHEN I BUILDED, HE DID PLAY ON THE SLIDE.
WHEN I RESTED, HE DID TELL ME THE LEGENDS OF THE BOY ANIMALS.
OF THOMAS TANKING-JOHN. OF SPIDER-BAT, AND INCREDIBLE HUCK.

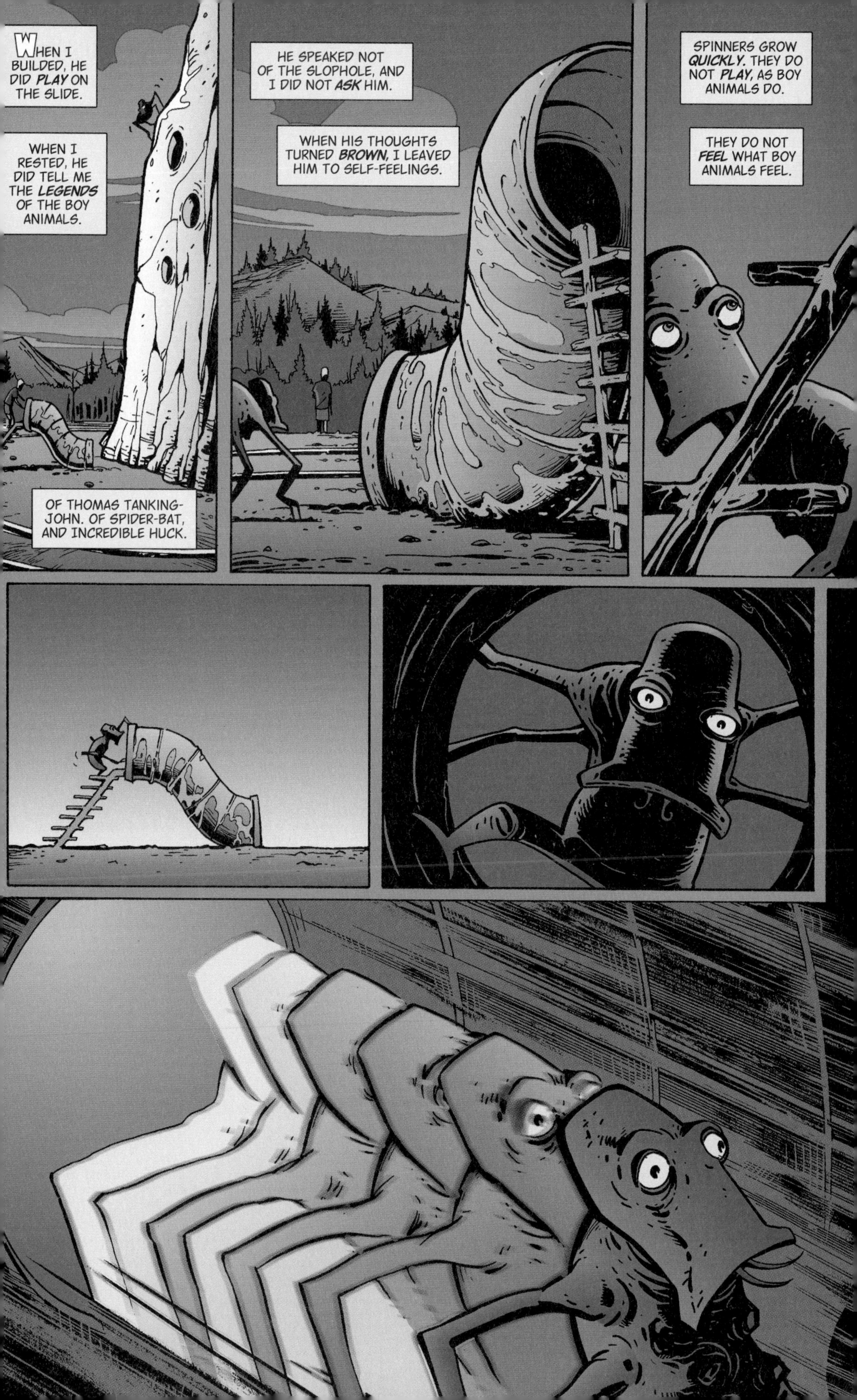

HE SPEAKED NOT OF THE SLOPHOLE, AND I DID NOT ASK HIM.
WHEN HIS THOUGHTS TURNED BROWN, I LEAVED HIM TO SELF-FEELINGS.

SPINNERS GROW QUICKLY. THEY DO NOT PLAY, AS BOY ANIMALS DO.
THEY DO NOT FEEL WHAT BOY ANIMALS FEEL.

WHUMP
LOVER.
I'M YOURS.

PUPPE
ONE SHOWING
HEATRO DE U.P.C.
TWO THOUSAND

SO THE WORD STARTED TO GET AROUND. WHATEVER GAME THE DEVIL'S PLAYING, IT'S GOT A NEW SET OF RULES.
NO GODS. NO DEMONS. NO FAIRIES, IFRITS, ELEMENTALS, AB-DEAD, CHTHONIC POWERS OR LAUGHING GNOMES.
IF YOU'RE IMMORTAL, YOUR VISA EXPIRED, LIKE, YESTERDAY.
The Winnowing
WIRE, BRIAR, LIMBER LOCK I
MIKE CAREY WRITER
PETER GROSS & RYAN KELLY ARTISTS
JARED FLETCHER-LETTERING
DANIEL VOZZO-COLORS AND SEPARATIONS
CHRISTOPHER MOELLER-COVER PAINTER
MARIAH HUEHNER-ASSISTANT EDITOR
SHELLY BOND-EDITOR
BASED ON CHARACTERS CREATED BY GAIMAN, KIETH AND DRINGENBERG
AND IF YOU THINK YOU MIGHT BE IMMORTAL, JUST ASK.
LUCIFER'S GOT A SUREFIRE WAY OF FINDING OUT.

Y'KNOW, I THINK WE COULD JUST *SIT* THIS OUT.
NONE OF THESE GUYS IS GOING TO STICK AROUND FOR THE *PUNCH LINE*.

UHH... SURE, MONA. THANKS FOR SHARING.
SO THE DOS AMIGOS RIDE AGAIN, RIGHT?
I'M SORRY, GAUDIUM. NOT THIS TIME.
I THOUGHT I'D TRAVEL WITH MAZIKEEN. AT LEAST TO BEGIN WITH.

THAT'S ABSURD. TO ENCUMBER THE BEST WARRIOR HERE WITH THE CARE OF A CHILD--
SHE IS A CHILD NO MORE, ELOKIM SHAER.
AND YOU WILL BE SILENT UNTIL I CALL ON YOU TO SPEAK.

I UNDERSTAND. YOU WANT MY STRENGTH, BUT YOU DON'T TRUST MY TEMPER.
IF I DIDN'T TRUST YOU, I WOULDN'T HAVE ASKED FOR YOUR HELP.
BUT IT'S TRUE THAT I WANT TO DO THIS WITHOUT HURTING ANYONE.

GAUDIUM, I NEED YOU TO LOOK AFTER MONA FOR ME.
OW! STOP IT! MY FUCKING SISTER'S WATCHING.
MY IMAGE WON'T STAND THIS KIND OF TREATMENT!

GOOD LUCK, ALL OF YOU. AND BE CAREFUL-- SINCE I'M BACK IN A REAL BODY I CAN'T WATCH OVER YOU.
BUT I'LL BE THINKING OF YOU. AND I'LL CHECK IN WHENEVER I CAN.

I CALLED IT ON THE MONEY-- BUT SO DID THE KID.
SHE'S WAY SHARP SINCE SHE DID THAT LAZARUS THING.
WITH MOST OF THESE SCHMUCKS WE'D JUST GO, "THE BIG GUY'S TAPPING HIS FOOT NOW."
AND THEY'D BE LIKE, "WE'RE GONE."
BUT THERE WERE HOLD-OUTS.
THE DEAF. THE DESPERATE. THE DUMB.
FUCK THAT NOISE. GIVEN THE ALTERNATIVE, WE WERE DOING THEM A FAVOR.
AND WE WERE READY FOR ALL THAT SHIT.
WE WERE READY FOR ANYTHING...

One Flew East...
OKAY. MY CHERUB-SENSE IS TINGLING.
WHAT DOES THAT MEAN?
IT MEANS THERE ARE DEMONS IN THIS HORSE-DEFICIENT STINKPIT.
SHOULD WE SPLIT UP AND LOOK AROUND?
SURE. YOU CHECK THE MIDDEN HEAPS, I'LL DO THE BARS AND THE STRIP CLUBS.
MESDAMES-- MESSIEURS-- MY LORDS, LADIES, AND LUSCIOUS LITTLE ONES--
--A THOUSAND THOUSAND WELCOMES TO Teatro Crepuscolo!
SMALLER THAN A SUITCASE! BIGGER THAN THE GRANDEST OPERA!
Teatro Crepuscolo WILL DAZZLE YOUR EYES AND CONFOUND YOUR EXPECTATIONS!

SEE, HERE IS A WORLD, LONG PAST ITS EST, THAT ONCE IN GREEN AND GOLD WAS SWEETLY DRESSED.
INTO THE APPLE CRAWLS THE SPITEFUL WORM. ALL THINGS THAT LIVE, IN DEATH MUST MEET THEIR TERM.
AND LONG ERE DEATH TO AGE AND ROT THEY BEND; IN PAIN AND SICKNESS YEARN TOWARDS THEIR END.
LOOK AT THE BLOOM THAT FADES FROM YOUR OWN CHEEKS.
TASTE THE FOUL BREATH THAT IN YOUR OWN THROAT REEKS.
REJOICE IN ALL THE WEALTH YOUR MAKER GAVE.
BRIEF LIFE, FALSE LOVE, LOST STRENGTH AND SHALLOW GRAVE.
YOU HAVE THE SENSE OF IT NOW. THE DESPAIR. THE UNBEARABLE WEIGHT OF IT.
YOU LONG TO LAY THAT WEIGHT DOWN. AND MESDAMES, MESSIEURS--

--Teatro Crepuscolo *NEVER* DISAPPOINTS!

!
THAT SOUNDED **NASTY.**

HISHHHH

EWWWWWWWWWW!

YOU!
ME?
YOU DID THIS! YOU KILLED ALL THESE PEOPLE!
I'M JUST A *PUPPET* THEATRE.
OH *SURE* YOU ARE.
POISON IN *JEST*-- NO OFFENSE IN THE WORLD.
YOU'RE THE DEMON.
YOU'RE JUST *WEARING* THAT THING SO YOU CAN GET UP CLOSE TO PEOPLE AND EAT THEM.
PLEASE, PETITE MAM'SELLE, PETIT BIJOU!
DO NOT JUMP TO ANY HASTY *CONCLUSIONS.*

THE TRAGICAL HISTORY OF MONA DOYLE--
A DRAMA IN *THREE* ACTS.
OH! OH! DADDY! DON'T TEAR MY MAGAZINE, PLEASE!
I'LL TEAR MORE THAN YOUR *MAGAZINE*, YOU SNIVELING LITTLE BITCH!
YOU'RE NOT MINE! EVERY TIME I LOOK AT YOU I SEE THAT IRISH SPUNKWAD LOOKING BACK AT ME!
HO HO HO! I WILL PUSH THIS LITTLE GIRL UNDER A CAR IN CASE SHE REVEALS HOW *EVIL* I AM.
NOBODY WILL *MISS* HER.
OH LOOK! A DISCARDED *SOUL* THAT NO ONE WANTS.
I'LL USE IT AS *BAIT* FOR ELAINE BELLOC. CERTAINLY IT HAS NO *OTHER* DISCERNIBLE FUNCTION.
THREE ACTS--
--AND AN *EPILOGUE.*

YOU NEVER *CHANGE,* ABRAZUL.
EVEN THE CHEESY *PICKUP* LINES ARE THE SAME.
GRAWWWWWWW!
KNOW YOUR *PLACE,* GAUDIUM! I'LL LEAVE YOU HER *BONES* TO CHEW ON!
NEWSFLASH, SNAKEFACE. THE KID'S WITH *ME.*

SQUITSCH

WHAT? WHAT ARE YOU *LOOKING* AT?

GAUDIUM! YOU WENT BACK TO YOUR *OLD* SHAPE.

THE ONE YOU HAD IN HEAVEN BEFORE--

CASE IN POINT--

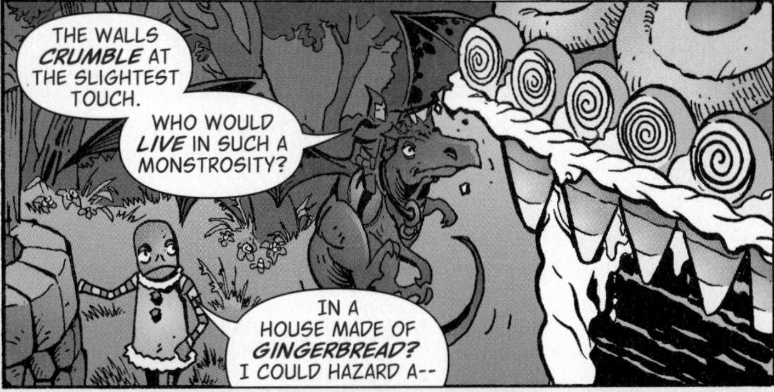
THE WALLS CRUMBLE AT THE SLIGHTEST TOUCH.
WHO WOULD LIVE IN SUCH A MONSTROSITY?
IN A HOUSE MADE OF GINGERBREAD? I COULD HAZARD A--

STOP!
ELOKIM SHAER, DON'T EAT THAT!

KRAKOOOOM

WHO'S THAT NIBBLING AT MY WALLS?
TWO CHERRY-CHEEKED LITTLE CHILDREN, IS IT, COME TO VISIT GRANDMA?
ARE YOU BLIND, OLD WOMAN?
WE'RE NOT CHILDREN. WE'RE NOT EVEN OF YOUR--
NOW, NOW, NOW, LITTLE BOY. GRANDMA IS OLD AND BENT--
--BUT SHE KNOWS A HAWK FROM A HANDSAW.
TWO DARLING LITTLE MORSELS. SO INNOCENT.
SO TENDER.

ARE YOU *AWAKE,* MY POPPETS?
SUCH *SLEEPY-HEADS* YOU ARE, AND THE SUN STILL HIGH IN THE SKY.

THERE, DOLLYKINS. PUSH THE STICKS TO THE BACK OF THE FIRE.
YOU'LL HAVE TO LEAN FORWARD ON TIPPY-TOES, BUT GRANDMA WILL HOLD YOU.
I'M SORRY, GRANDMA--
--BUT THIS BULLSHIT HAS GONE ON LONG ENOUGH.
WHAT?
YOU'LL DO AS YOU'RE TOLD, MY FINE LITTLE MADAM.
OR ELSE YOU'LL FEEL HOW HEAVY GRANDMA'S HAND CAN BE.
YOU GOT THE COTTAGE RIGHT, BUT THIS IS SOME KIND OF HALLOWEEN OUTFIT.
AND GRETEL TRICKED THE WITCH INTO THE OVEN, NOT THE OTHER WAY AROUND.
IT'S BEEN A WHILE SINCE YOU HEARD THIS STORY, HASN'T IT?

URRRRRRR!

THAT'S THE WAY *I* REMEMBER THE STORY TOO.
NO, IT WAS ***KLUGE HANS!***
SHE ***CAN'T*** PUT US IN THE FIRE! I WON'T GO!

THERE ARE A ***THOUSAND*** SOULS INSIDE HER. I SEE THEM NOW.
STRIKE, WHILE THEY'RE AT ***ODDS*** WITH EACH OTHER!
GRANDMA-- I KNOW WHO YOU ***ARE.***

YOU DON'T YOU DON'T YOU DON'T!
I'M THE WICKED ***WITCH*** AND I'LL KILL YOU!

UHHH! GRANDMA, SHOULDN'T--
--SHOULDN'T THE CHILDREN LIVE--
--HAPPILY EVER AFTER?
YOU DON'T-- HAVE TO STAY HERE.
YOU DON'T HAVE TO BE SCARED ANY-MORE.

THE CHILDREN FROM THE WELL--?
YEAH. HUNDREDS OF MISERABLE LITTLE GHOSTS, CLINGING TOGETHER.
DISGUISED AS THE SCARIEST THING THEY COULD THINK OF.

WHY DID THEY NEED A DISGUISE?

WELL, SOMETHING KILLED THEM AND MADE THEM INTO A WATER FEATURE.
MAYBE THAT HAD SOMETHING TO DO WITH IT.

THEY WANTED TO MAKE ALL THE BAD THINGS KEEP THEIR DISTANCE. AND LET'S FACE IT--
WHAM
--IT'S NOT LIKE THEY HAD A CHOICE OF SCENIC DESTINATIONS.

YOU SEEM ANGRY.
OF COURSE I'M ANGRY. SLOPPY WORK ALWAYS MAKES ME ANGRY.

WHO BUILDS A CREATION AND THEN LEAVES OUT THE AFTERLIFE?

LIKE FATHER, LIKE SON.

IT'S ALWAYS SOMEONE ELSE WHO HAS TO TAKE UP THE FUCKING SLACK.
WITCH'S KOTTAGE

One Flew Over the Cuckoo's Nest...
WHERE NEXT?
GIVE ME A MINUTE OR TWO, MAZIKEEN. PLEASE.
AS FAR AS THE MOUNTAINS THERE'S NOTHING. NOTHING LIVES HERE.
THEN WE SHOULD MOVE ON.
WE WILL. I'M JUST A BIT TIRED.
IT'S BEEN A LONG TIME SINCE I HAD A BODY. I'M STILL NOT QUITE--

SLEEP, ELAINE BELLOC.
WE *MISSED* ONE.
I'LL DEAL WITH IT.

THE WORLD WAS LOOKING STRANGE.
NOT JUST UPSIDE DOWN, BUT DIM, AND A BIT RED AROUND THE EDGES.
LIKE CARPETS.
I HEARD YOUR **CALL,** SEX-BLOSSOM.
HERE I **AM.**
AND IT SMELLED REAL BAD.
CARPETS THAT HAD GOT WET AND THEN GOT DRY AGAIN.
YOU **COMED!** YOU COMED AT LAST TO ME!
MOST BEAUTEOUS! MOST FECUND! SCARCELY CAN I CONTAIN MY **JOY!**
KISS MY **KNUCKLES.** I LIKE THAT.
BUT THE BOY MARTIN. I WOULD ASK YOU PLEASE TO **RELEASE** HIM.
HE IS MY **FRIEND.**
FRIEND?
HNN.

WELL LET'S SEE THIS HOUSE OF YOURS. IF I LIKE IT, YOU CAN FEED ME.
THEN YOU CAN FUCK ME.
HEY, YOU MADE MY NOSE BLEED. YOU SHOULDN'T'VE--
KERRUNCH
The War
STITCHGLASS SLIDE II
MIKE CAREY WRITER
PETER GROSS & RYAN KELLY ARTISTS
JARED FLETCHER-LETTERING
DANIEL VOZZO-COLORS AND SEPARATIONS
CHRISTOPHER MOELLER-COVER PAINTER
MARIAH HUEHNER-ASSISTANT EDITOR
SHELLY BOND-EDITOR
BASED ON CHARACTERS CREATED BY GAIMAN, KIETH AND DRINGENBERG
...

HERE DOES BE THE EGG CHAMBER. I WEAVED IT FROM--
MAYBE YOU DIDN'T HEAR ME, SUGAR LUMP.
I SAID I'M HUNGRY.
UUNA WILL WAIT IN THE FOODPIT.
SHE LIKES SWEET POTATOES, NUTMEG, SPEARGRASS, WILD THYME AND CACTUS ROOTS. AND TO HAVE HER ARMPITS LICKED WHILE SHE EATS.
POOR THOLE! THIS WAS WHAT HE'D BEEN BUILDING UP TO ALL THIS TIME.
WITH UUNA AND HIS HORMONES ALL GANGING UP ON HIM, HE DIDN'T HAVE A CHANCE.
BUT ALL I COULD SEE WAS THAT HE WAS IGNORING ME.
SHE SMASHED MY SLIDE, AND HE WAS RUNNING AFTER HER!
WELL HE'D BE SORRY.
THEY'D BOTH BE SORRY.
BUT WHEN THEY SAID THEY WERE SORRY I'D TELL THEM IT WAS TOO LATE.

SOMETHING WAS DIGGING INTO MY LEG. SOMETHING IN MY POCKET.
A MARBLE?
A JAWBREAKER?
THE SELF-STONE.
THOLE'S FIRST GIFT TO ME.
WELL, I DIDN'T WANT ANYTHING OFF OF HIM!
I UPPED AND I THREW IT, AS FAR AWAY AS I COULD, AND I--
STOPPED
BEING
ME
IMAGINE A SYMPHONY THAT'S ALL CRESCENDO.
IMAGINE A TIDE THAT NEVER GOES OUT.

THOLE HAD WOVEN HIS HOUSE OUT OF MILLIONS OF STRANDS OF EMOTION-- THIN, BUT STRONG, LIKE WIRE.
ONCE I LET GO OF THE SELF-STONE, EVERY ONE OF THOSE WIRES WAS PUMPING ITS CURRENT DIRECTLY INTO ME.
THE HUNGER OF THE PREDATOR. THE FEAR OF THE PREY.
THE ANGER, LOVE, PAIN AND JOY OF COUNTLESS MINDS, ALL SPUN TOGETHER LIKE FLAX.
AND LIKE BASS NOTES PLUCKED FROM MY OWN INTESTINES, THE SORROW OF THE IMMORTALS--
--DRIVEN FORTH FROM THIS REALM BY LUCIFER'S EDICT, HARRIED BY HIS SERVANTS--
FRIEND MARTIN, YOU MUST HELP ME TO HUNT FOR WILD STRAWBERRIES AND BLOODWEED.
UUNA IS STILL HUNGRY!

THAT FIRST DAY WAS BAD. BUT IT GOT WORSE.
UUNA RULED NOW. AND THOLE DOTED ON HER LIKE A LOVESICK PUPPY.
AFTER A COUPLE OF BAD EXPERIENCES WITH HER HEAVY HANDS AND SHORT TEMPER, I KEPT OUT OF HER WAY.
EVERY TIME SHE SMELLED ME, SHE GROWLED LIKE SHE HAD A TOOTHACHE OR SOMETHING.
I KNEW JUST ENOUGH ABOUT SEX TO KNOW THAT WHEN THEY'D DONE IT THE EGGS WOULD BE FULL OF SOMETHING.
I CHECKED THEM EVERY DAY. THEY STAYED EMPTY.
BUT THEN UUNA STARTED PUTTING ON WEIGHT-- WHICH WAS PRETTY SCARY TO SEE.
SHE STOPPED MOVING AROUND. JUST STAYED IN THE FOODPIT ALL THE TIME AND ATE. AND THEN ONE DAY--
--SHE CAUGHT MY SCENT ON HER LOLLING TONGUE, AND SMILED.
MARTINNN...
OR AT ANY RATE, SHE SHOWED HER TEETH.

I THINK I'LL BE SQUIRTING SOME YOLKS INTO THOSE EGGS OF YOURS PRETTY SOON.
MOST BLISSFUL OF ALL DAYS! MOST WELCOME OF ANY NEWS!
SO I'M STARTING TO HANKER. YOU KNOW ABOUT HANKERING?
I HAVE HEARD OF IT. SHALL I MASSAGE YOUR SCALP SOME MORE?
NO, MY LITTLE FUCK-FLOWER.
JUST BRING ME THE BOY.

I REALLY, REALLY DIDN'T WANT TO DO THIS.
THERE'D BE SO MANY QUESTIONS. SO MANY EXPLANATIONS TO GET THROUGH...
AND SOMEWHERE IN THE CLUTTER AT THE BOTTOM OF MY HEART WAS ANOTHER FEAR.
THAT ONCE THEY'D GOT ME BACK, MY MOM AND DAD WOULD NEVER LET ME GO AGAIN.
...
I DIDN'T UNDERSTAND BACK THEN ABOUT THE GATES.
NOW YOU QUIT FOOLING AROUND, MARTIN, AND GET BACK DOWNSTAIRS.
HOW A WHOLE RIVER OF TIME COULD ROLL BY ON ONE SIDE OF THEM--
--AND ON THE OTHER SIDE, JUST A TRICKLE.
LIKE COLD SWEAT.
OR A TEAR.

THOLE!
I'VE GOT SOME FOOD STUCK BETWEEN MY TEETH.
I WILL SCRAPE IT AWAY MOMENTLY.
WITH A TWIG OF FRAGRANT EUCALYPTUS.
YOU MISS THE BOY ANIMAL?
IT GRIEVES ME THAT HE GOED AWAY SO SUDDENLY.
BUT IF HE HAD STAYED, YOU WOULD HAVE DEVOURED HIM--
AND THAT WOULD HAVE HURTED ME MORE.
HNNNN.

I MISS HIM, TOO.
HAVE THAT EUCALYPTUS TWIG READY FOR WHEN I GET BACK.
I GO WHERE I LIKE.
YOU KNOW, SPUNK-MUFFIN, I'VE CHANGED MY MIND.
NO NO NO NO NO!
THIS THING MUST NOT BE! YOU CANNOT GO THERE!
NNNNGGG!
BOIL SOME WATER, AND TIDY UP THAT FOODPIT.
WE'RE GOING TO EAT THE LITTLE BASTARD TOGETHER.

I FOUND HIM HIDING IN THE ATTIC. SORRY ABOUT THE INCONVENIENCE, MR. ROUSSEAU.
THERE'S NO INCONVENIENCE.
MARTIN, WHAT DID YOU DO TO YOUR CLOTHES?
I GUESS I SCARED YOU, DIDN'T I, MARTIN?
NO!
YOU HURT MY HEAD!
I KNOW I DID. AND BELIEVE ME, I'M SORRY IT HAS TO HURT.
BUT IT'S LIKE-- DAYLIGHT HURTS YOUR EYES WHEN YOU'VE BEEN LIVING IN THE DARK. YOU SEE?
AGILE
WHAT WAS THAT?
BOXES. HE HAD THEM ALL STACKED UP.
I GUESS THEY OVERBALANCED.
ANYWAY, YOU COME ON OVER HERE.
AND WE'LL JUST TAKE UP WHERE WE LEFT OFF.

KER-R-RACKKK

YOU KNOW, IN MY CONDITION--

--YOU SHOULDN'T B MAKING ME D THINGS LIKE THIS.

AND ON THE FAR SIDE OF THE GATE, THE RIVER RAN *ON.*
THOLE *WAITED,* TENSE AND TERRIFIED AND IRRESOLUTE.
THE LONG DAY WANED. THE SLOW MOON CLIMBED. HE *FOUGHT* AGAINST HIMSELF.
AGAINST HIS *LOVE,* WHICH HAD BEEN THE POINT OF HIS EXISTENCE.
THE NEXT MORNING, HE BEGAN TO *BUILD.*
GLISSADES OF WEAKNESS. TERRACES OF GUILT AND SHAME.
AMBUSCADES.
STITCHGLASS *WAR.*

HNN. YOU'VE BEEN BUSY.
WELL DONE, LOVER. THIS IS ALMOST CLEVER.
THOOOOM
BUT I SAW IT COMING.
YOU CAN'T MESS WITH MY FEELINGS--
--UNLESS THIS STUFF ACTUALLY TOUCHES ME.

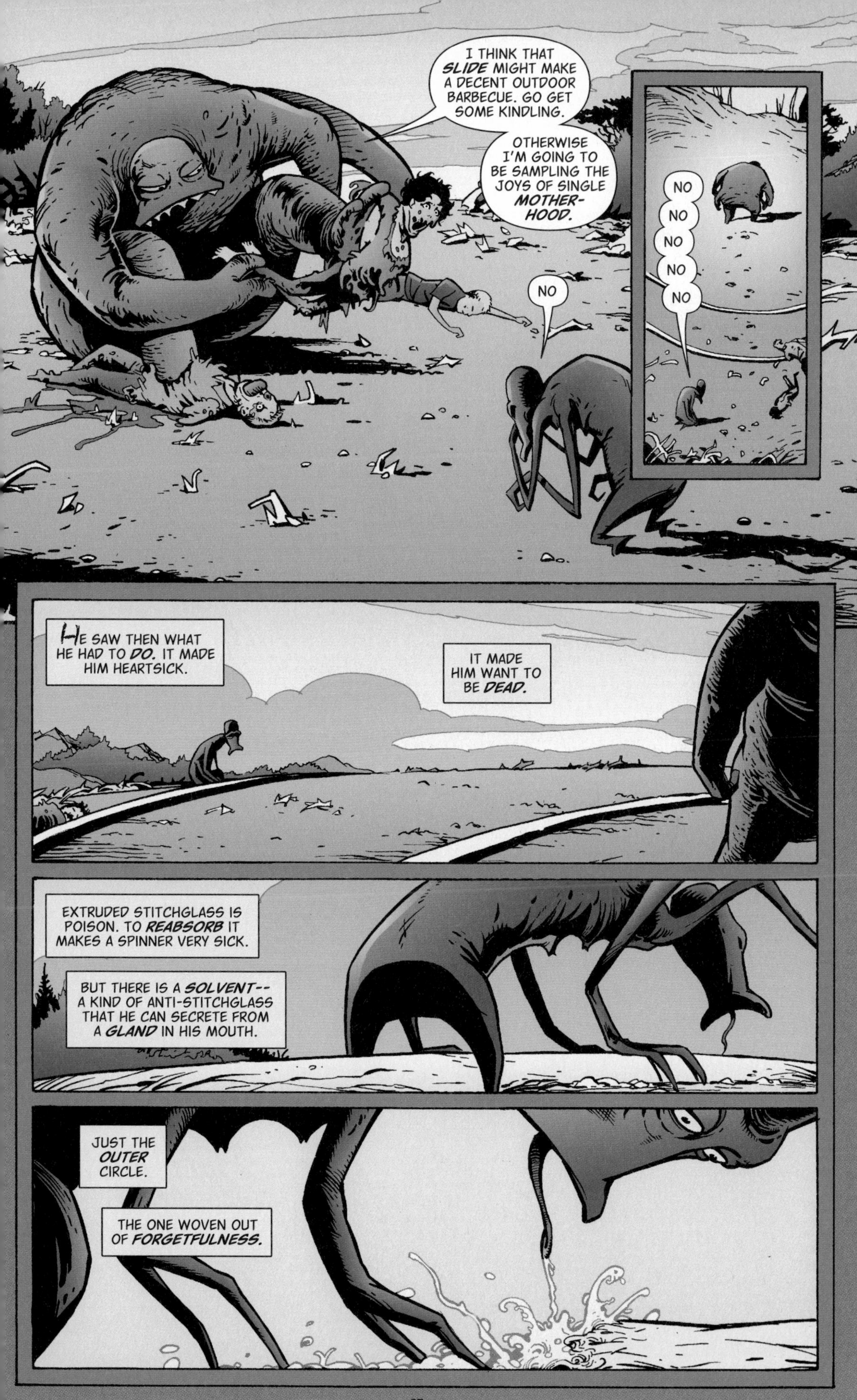
I THINK THAT SLIDE MIGHT MAKE A DECENT OUTDOOR BARBECUE. GO GET SOME KINDLING.
OTHERWISE I'M GOING TO BE SAMPLING THE JOYS OF SINGLE MOTHER-HOOD.
NO
NO
NO
NO
NO
NO
HE SAW THEN WHAT HE HAD TO DO. IT MADE HIM HEARTSICK.
IT MADE HIM WANT TO BE DEAD.
EXTRUDED STITCHGLASS IS POISON. TO REABSORB IT MAKES A SPINNER VERY SICK.
BUT THERE IS A SOLVENT-- A KIND OF ANTI-STITCHGLASS THAT HE CAN SECRETE FROM A GLAND IN HIS MOUTH.
JUST THE OUTER CIRCLE.
THE ONE WOVEN OUT OF FORGETFULNESS.

SLEEP, ELAINE BELLOC.
HE WAS SENDING UP A SIGNAL FLARE.
I DON'T KNOW WHO HE THOUGHT WOULD ANSWER IT.
BUT AS IT TURNED OUT, THERE WAS ONE IN THE WASTELAND WHO WATCHED--
--AND WAS MINDFUL OF US.
WE *MISSED* ONE.
I'LL DEAL WITH IT.

YOU. SPINNER.
ALL IMMORTALS WERE TOLD TO LEAVE THIS REALM. WHY ARE YOU STILL HERE?
I'M TRYING TO EAT.
AND ONLY OUR MENFOLK SPIN STITCH-GLASS.
THAT DOESN'T CONCERN ME.
AS I SAID--
WE FEMALES PREFER TO SQUIRT. THAT'S CONFUSION, BY THE WAY.
WITH A LITTLE FEAR.

CHOKE ON IT, YOU LILIM BITCH!
THINK YOU'RE TOO GOOD FOR THE REST OF US.
WHEN ALL YOU REALLY ARE--
--IS WEAK
SUFFERING
FLESH!

YOU BROKE THE *EGGS!*
I WAS NEVER THE MOTHERLY *TYPE,* BUT I'M STILL GOING TO RIP YOUR--
GUUUUUUH!

AND YOU? YOU CAN LEAVE OR YOU CAN DIE.
DECIDE NOW. I'VE WASTED ENOUGH TIME ALREADY.
I-- I--
MAZIKEEN.
YOU SHOULD HAVE WOKEN ME.

WHY? I WAS CARRYING OUT MY ORDERS.
LET HIM CHOOSE, AND THEN WE'RE DONE HERE.
CHOOSE WHAT?
DEATH, OR EXILE.
AS MY LORD LUCIFER HAS DECREED.
WELL LET'S SEE...
WHAT HE ACTUALLY SAID WAS THAT ALL THE IMMORTALS HAD TO LEAVE.
THOLE?
THAT IS YOUR NAME, RIGHT?
HOW SOLD ARE YOU ON IMMORTALITY?
I MEAN, AS A CONCEPT?

IT WAS ELAINE. ONE OF THE HOLY SISTERS.
WHO HER COMPANION WAS, I NEVER FOUND OUT. AND THE MEMORY OF WHAT SHE DID TO THOLE REMAINS SHADOWY AND INCOMPLETE WITHIN MY MIND.
BUT AFTERWARDS THEY LEFT WITHOUT A WORD.
LEFT US TO MOURN, AND TRY TO UNDERSTAND.
I LIVED IN THAT PLACE FOR FOURTEEN YEARS.
IT BECAME MY HOME, AND THOLE BECAME MY FATHER-- EACH MORE PRECIOUS TO THE OTHER BECAUSE OF WHAT WE'D LOST.
I CANNOT SAY MY HEART BROKE WHEN HE DIED. I HAD WATCHED HIM GROW OLD, AND I AM A REALIST ABOUT SUCH THINGS.
AS A REALIST I SAT AND PONDERED ON WHAT HE HAD GIVEN UP TO STAY WITH ME.
TO GIVE ME A HOME.
THE GRIEF ITSELF I BALANCE WITHIN ME. AS HE WOULD HAVE DONE.
UNTIL I CAN WEAVE IT INTO SOMETHING ELSE.

SHE DOES NOT SPEAK AS WE COME AWAY.
SHE IS ANGRY.
IT SHOWS IN HER FACE, FIRST--
--THEN IN HER BODY--
--AND FINALLY IN HER WORLD.
The Widow
WIRE, BRIAR, LIMBER LOCK II
MIKE CAREY WRITER
PETER GROSS & RYAN KELLY ARTISTS
JARED FLETCHER-LETTERING
DANIEL VOZZO-COLORS AND SEPARATIONS
CHRISTOPHER MOELLER-COVER PAINTER
MARIAH HUEHNER-ASSISTANT EDITOR
SHELLY BOND-EDITOR
BASED ON CHARACTERS CREATED BY
GAIMAN, KIETH AND DRINGENBERG

MAZIKEEN, DON'T DO THAT AGAIN. FIGHT AND KILL WITHOUT--
--WITHOUT EVEN TELLING ME FIRST.
VERY WELL. I WILL NOT.
BUT I THINK THERE MAY BE OTHER THINGS THAT HAVE PROVOKED THIS ANGER, ELAINE BELLOC.
AND IF YOU DON'T CONTROL IT, THE LAND WILL SUFFER.
YOU'RE RIGHT. AND I'M SORRY.
FOR WHAT? MY LORD LUCIFER HAS COMMANDED ME TO OBEY YOU.
IF I ERR, I MUST BE TOLD.
AS THE GROUND BEGINS TO RISE AGAIN, WE LEAVE THE BOY AND THE STITCHGLASS SPINNER BEHIND US.
THEY ARE BOTH MORTAL NOW. AND WE WERE TOLD TO WEED OUT THOSE WHO DO NOT DIE.

SHE SAYS AT LAST.
THEY WERE THE BOY'S PARENTS.

THE BODIES. WE LEFT HIM DIGGING A *GRAVE* FOR HIS MUM AND DAD.

AND IT WAS *THAT* WHICH MOVED YOU?
THE OTHER WAY *AROUND* IS USUALLY CONSIDERED MORE TRAGIC.

I SUPPOSE.
IT JUST REMINDED ME OF-- STUFF THAT I'D *FORGOTTEN.*
STUFF THAT I'D *LET* MYSELF FORGET.
YOUR *OWN* DEATH.

NO, THAT SORT OF *STAYS* WITH YOU. I WAS THINKING ABOUT MATT AND BARBARA. AND DAVID EASTERMAN.

ALL THE PEOPLE WHO THOUGHT THEY WERE *MY* PARENTS.

I WISH I'D KNOWN MORE BACK THEN ABOUT WHAT I WAS.
ENOUGH TO *PROTECT* THEM, MAYBE.
PROTECT THEM FROM *WHAT?*

WELL... FROM *LIFE.* FROM ALL THE STUFF THAT THEY WERE SUPPOSED TO PROTECT *ME* FROM.

IT'S HARD TO *EXPLAIN.* DID YOU HAVE A YOUNGER BROTHER OR SISTER? SOMEONE YOU WERE SUPPOSED TO LOOK OUT FOR?

I HAD MANY THOUSANDS OF EACH. IT'S WHY I VALUE MY *PRIVACY.*
OKAY. THEN HOW ABOUT LUCIFER?
THE WAY YOU WATCH *HIS* BACK. ISN'T THAT KIND OF LIKE--?

THWIIIP

FOR ALL HER *POWER,* SHE DIDN'T SENSE THAT WE WERE OBSERVED.
DID I JUST *MISS* SOME-THING?
YES.
THAT SOMETHING WAS MOVING, IN THE DARK BEYOND THE CAMPFIRE.

SOMETHING THAT COULD OUTRUN MY DAGGER. WELL, NO MATTER.
TO BE AWARE OF A THREAT IS TO REPLY TO IT. FOR ME--
--AS FOR MY MASTER.

LOS ANGELES.
THE HOUSE OF LUCIFER MORNINGSTAR.
I SEE YOU'VE COME ARMED.
I SHOULD HAVE SPECIFIED SEMI-FORMAL.
THE HOST ARE MINDFUL OF THE HELP YOU LATELY OFFERED US, LUCIFER.
BUT STILL YOU ARE THE ADVERSARY.
AND IF I TURN NASTY YOU WANT TO DIE WITH YOUR BOOTS ON. I SEE.
DID YOU CALL US HERE TO INSULT US?
NO, URIEL-- TO WARN YOU. I THOUGHT YOU SHOULD HAVE TIME TO PREPARE.
PREPARE FOR WHAT?
FOR THE END OF THE WORLD.
COME AND SEE.

WELL, WE'RE FINISHED HERE. THE LAST IMMORTALS ARE GONE.
I'VE CAST MY MIND OUT CLEAR ACROSS THOSE MOUNTAINS AND THERE'S NOTHING THERE.
GOOD. THIS WORK HAS SEEMED INTERMINABLE.
YOU'VE GOT SOMEWHERE ELSE YOU NEED TO BE, MAZIKEEN? YOU SHOULD HAVE SAID.
HERE. LET'S SEE WHAT I CAN WHIP UP FOR YOU.

YOU SEE THE *CLEARING?*
OF COURSE.
SET DOWN THERE. THE OTHERS ARE *WAITING* FOR US.

MONA! YOU'RE OKAY! I WAS WORRIED ABOUT YOU.
I'M FINE. I HAD GAUDIUM TO LOOK AFTER ME.
FEH.
HERE'S THE FINAL SCORE. TWELVE THOUSAND SEVEN HUNDRED AND TWENTY-TWO EVICTIONS, SEVENTY-FOUR FATALITIES.
THANKS, SPERA. I'LL LOOK AT IT LATER.
SO THE GOOD GUYS WON. ARE WE HOT, OR ARE WE NOT?
ALL ASSES KICKED-- NO JOB TOO BIG OR TOO SMALL!
UMM... ACTUALLY IT OUGHT TO BE YOU DEALING OUT THE STROKES.
I KNOW.
FEEL FREE TO BUTT IN WITH THE OCCASIONAL ADJECTIVE.
I'M SORRY, GAUDIUM.
I JUST CAN'T FEEL VERY PROUD OF WHAT WE'VE DONE.
THAT CAME OUT WRONG. I'M GRATEFUL TO ALL OF YOU.
AND THE WAY YOU WORKED TOGETHER, AS A TEAM, WAS AMAZING.
I THINK WE ALL KNOW EACH OTHER-- TRUST EACH OTHER-- A LOT BETTER NOW.

BUT?
BUT MOST OF THE IMMORTALS WERE JUST MINDING THEIR OWN BUSINESS.
AND WE HOUNDED THEM AND CHASED THEM AWAY AND IF THEY DIDN'T GO WE KILLED THEM.
WE ONLY KILLED THE ONES WHO WERE TRYING TO KILL US, ELAINE.
WE DID WHAT WE UNDERTOOK TO DO.
TO A SOLDIER, THAT IN ITSELF IS VIRTUE.
AND YOU SHOULD ASK YOURSELF THIS. WOULD THOSE WHO DIED BE ALIVE NOW, IF MY LORD LUCIFER HAD VISITED THEM INSTEAD?
OR WOULD SOME OF THE LIVING NOW BE--
WHAT'S THE MATTER?
THE TREES--
THE TREES ARE TOO CLOSE.

TOO CLOSE?
WHAT, YOU WANT WE SHOULD MOVE THE FOREST BACK A WAYS?
WAIT. I THINK--
I THINK I MADE A MISTAKE.
OR ELSE SOMEONE WAS HIDING FROM--
UUUF!

HOLY MOTHER OF FUCK!
ELAINE!
SPREAD OUT. WE NEED TO--
THWIKKK
WHAT ARE YOU SMILING ABOUT?
I DIDN'T MISS LAST NIGHT.
MY PRIDE IS SALVAGED.

I THOUGHT YOU HAD DIVIDED YOUR GATEWAY INTO PIECES, MORNINGSTAR.
AND SPREAD THE PIECES AMONG THE WORLDS AND REALMS.
THAT'S RIGHT. I DID.
BUT THE GATEWAY BEARS MY FATHER'S IMPRIMATUR. IT'S INFINITE.
IF YOU DIVIDE INFINITY, YOU DON'T MAKE IT ANY SMALLER.
YOU SAID WE WERE TO SEE FOR OURSELVES.
SO FAR I'VE SEEN NOTHING TO IMPRESS ME.
WELL, THE OBSERVER IS PART OF THE SYSTEM, I SUPPOSE. BUT IF YOU KEEP WATCHING THE GATE--
FSSSSSSH

DOES--
DOES THAT HAPPEN OFTEN?
NO. BUT THE LETTERS OF MY FATHER'S NAME ARE ALL THAT HOLD THE GATE OPEN.
NOW HE'S GONE. AND YESTERDAY THE LETTERS BEGAN TO FADE.

TO--
FADE?
WITH THE RESULTS YOU SEE. I DOUBT THE GATE WILL LAST MORE THAN A FEW DAYS. A WEEK AT MOST.
SO YOUR REALM WILL BE SEPARATED FROM TRUE CREATION. IS THIS YOUR CRISIS?

I DON'T HAVE A CRISIS. I'M TELLING YOU THIS AS A SIMPLE COURTESY. YAHWEH'S NAME IS WRITTEN ON EVERY ATOM OF HIS CREATION.
IT'S THE GLUE THAT HOLDS REALITY TOGETHER. AND WHEN IT'S GONE--

--YOU WILL BE TOO.
ALONG WITH EVERYTHING ELSE THAT LIVES HERE.

IN A MELEE THE BASIC MANEUVER IS TO STRIKE AND SHIFT FOOTING.
YOU LET YOUR ENEMY EXPOSE HIS WEAKNESSES, AND THEN YOU PLAY ON THEM.
GIVEN THE CHOICE--
--YOU DO NOT FIGHT ON HIS HOME GROUND.
YES. I CAN-- SEE IT. STUPID. STUPID TO MISS SOMETHING SO--
--BIG.

YOU'RE THE GUARDIAN OF THE GREEN. THE SPIRIT OF ALL THAT HAS ROOTS AND GROWS.
I-- I AM. AND YOU ARE ELAINE, OF THE SISTERS!
YOU HID YOURSELF FROM US SO WELL. YOURSELF-- AND SOMEONE ELSE.
THE WIDOW. THE KERA THEODMET. SHE IS MY FRIEND AND MY PROTECTOR.
I LOVE HER. LEAVE HER BE, AND I PROMISE THIS WILL END.
SPIRIT--
--THIS HAS ALREADY ENDED.

YOU'RE SO YOUNG. I GUESS BECAUSE THE WHOLE WORLD IS YOUNG.
SPIRIT, THE MAKER HAS ORDERED ALL THE IMMORTALS TO LEAVE HIS REALM. YOU'VE GOT TO GO FROM THIS PLACE.
I CANNOT GO FROM THIS PLACE, BECAUSE I AM THIS PLACE!
I KNOW WHAT THE MAKER HAS SAID. BUT I DIE WHETHER I STAY OR GO!
AND IN THE GREEN--
--ISN'T DEATH PART OF THE WAY THINGS WORK?
YES. IT IS. BUT I WAS AFRAID BECAUSE I HAVE NOT KNOWN DEATH BEFORE.
AND I WANTED TO HELP THE KERA. BUT I AM READY NOW, ELAINE.

WHAT'S *HAPPENING* HERE?
AUTUMN.
JUST... AUTUMN.

THE GUARDIAN SPIRIT OF THIS WORLD'S PLANT LIFE JUST *DIED.*
THE FOREST'S *MOURNING* FOR HIM.

AND THERE'S *ANOTHER* IMMORTAL UP AHEAD OF US. HE WAS HIDING HER TOO.
HE CALLED HER THE *KERA*--SOMETHING.
THEODMET? THE KERA THEODMET?

I WOULD SPEAK WITH YOU, ELAINE BELLOC.
THE REST OF YOU WAIT HERE.
OH. RIGHT. CAN WE TALK AMONGST *OURSELVES?*

WE ASCEND THE FLANKS OF THE MOUNTAIN. PAST THE TREE LINE.
I AM AWARE OF ELAINE BELLOC'S EYES ON MY BACK. OF THE QUESTIONS SHE HAS NOT YET ASKED.
TO BE AN ONLY CHILD-- THAT CREATES A DIFFERENT KIND OF BOND, PERHAPS.
THE LILIM ARE MORE A NATION THAN A FAMILY. THE LOYALTY WE FEEL FOR EACH OTHER IS TRIBAL.
I GUESS I'M STARTING TO SEE HOW THAT WOULD WORK.
I'M MEANT TO BE LOOKING OUT FOR EVERY-BODY HERE. NOT THAT I'M DOING SUCH A GREAT JOB OF IT.
THIS JUST GOT PERSONAL, DIDN'T IT?
I BELIEVE--
YES.
THIS LAST ONE IS FOR ME TO DEAL WITH. LET ME DO IT ALONE--
--AND I WILL SAY NOTHING TO LUCIFER ABOUT WHAT YOU DID IN THE FOREST.

IT'S NO SECRET. I TOOK A CUTTING.
I KNOW.
SO HE CAN LIVE AGAIN SOMEWHERE ELSE. SOME DAY.
IF I TELL LUCIFER THE JOB'S DONE, AND THEN IT TURNS OUT NOT TO BE--
--HE'S LIKELY TO LOSE HIS SENSE OF HUMOR.
YOU WILL NOT SUFFER FOR MY DERELICTION.
I WILL SWEAR ON MY SWORD IF YOU REQUIRE IT, AND MY WORD IS--
TAKE IT AS READ. BE CAREFUL, MAZIKEEN.
YOU'RE SURLY AND SCARY AND I'VE HAD A LOUSY TIME WORKING WITH YOU.

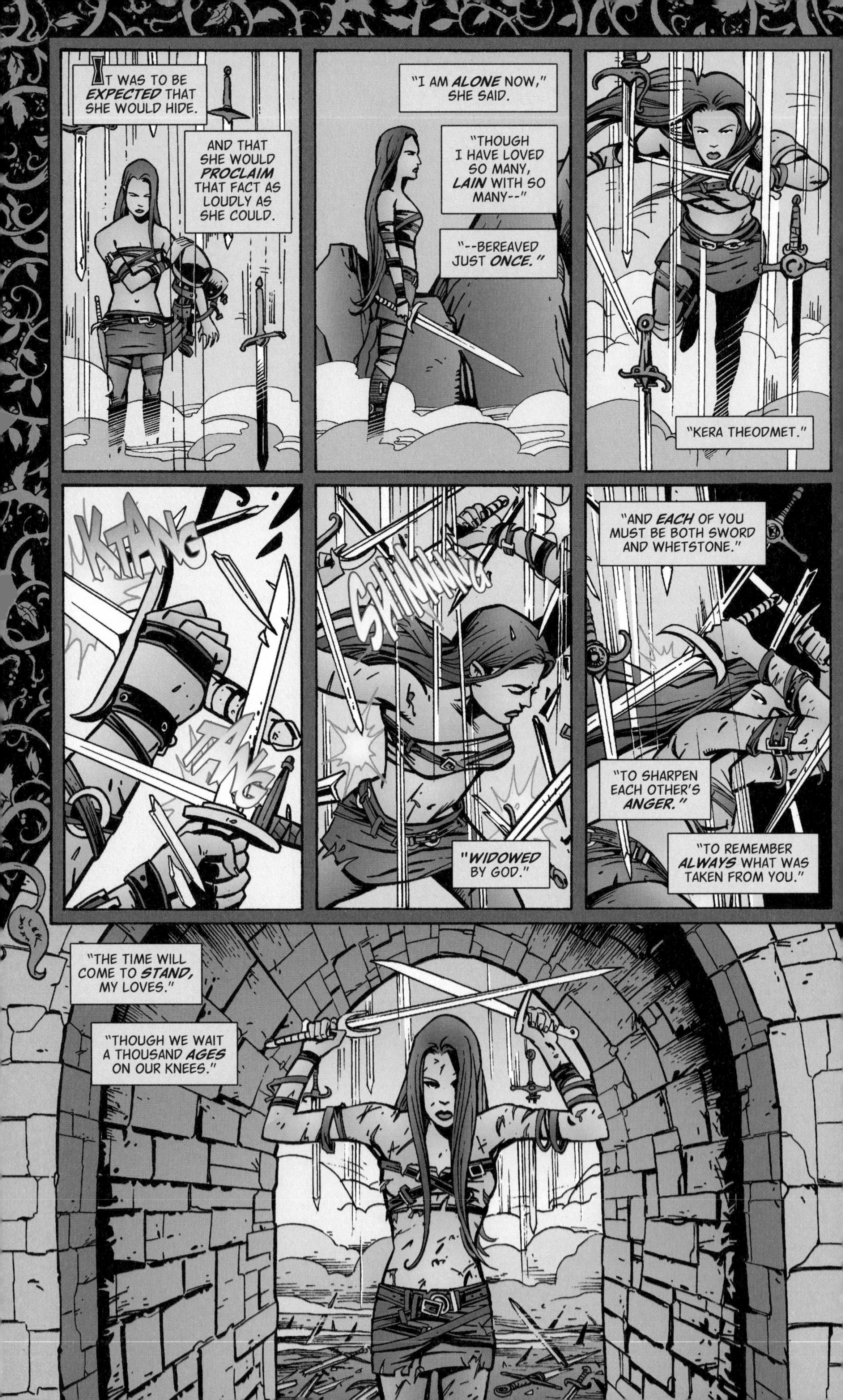
IT WAS TO BE EXPECTED THAT SHE WOULD HIDE.
AND THAT SHE WOULD PROCLAIM THAT FACT AS LOUDLY AS SHE COULD.
"I AM ALONE NOW," SHE SAID.
"THOUGH I HAVE LOVED SO MANY, LAIN WITH SO MANY--"
"--BEREAVED JUST ONCE."
"KERA THEODMET."
KTANG
TANG
SHINNNNG
"WIDOWED BY GOD."
"AND EACH OF YOU MUST BE BOTH SWORD AND WHETSTONE."
"TO SHARPEN EACH OTHER'S ANGER."
"TO REMEMBER ALWAYS WHAT WAS TAKEN FROM YOU."
"THE TIME WILL COME TO STAND, MY LOVES."
"THOUGH WE WAIT A THOUSAND AGES ON OUR KNEES."

THIS DOESN'T LOOK MUCH LIKE THE INSIDE OF A *MOUNTAIN.*
NO.
AND THAT DOES NOT SOUND MUCH LIKE *LOVE,* OR DUTY.
I EXPECTED *MORE,* AFTER SO LONG A PARTING.
YOU EXPECT TOO *MUCH,* MOTHER.
YOU ALWAYS *DID.*

Lilith
MIKE CAREY
WRITER
P. CRAIG RUSSELL
ARTIST
BASED ON CHARACTERS
CREATED BY
GAIMAN, KIETH & DRINGENBERG
JARED FLETCHER-LETTERING
LOVERN KINDZIERSKI-COLORS AND SEPARATIONS
CHRISTOPHER MOELLER-COVER PAINTER
MARIAH HUEHNER-ASSISTANT EDITOR
SHELLY BOND-EDITOR
2004

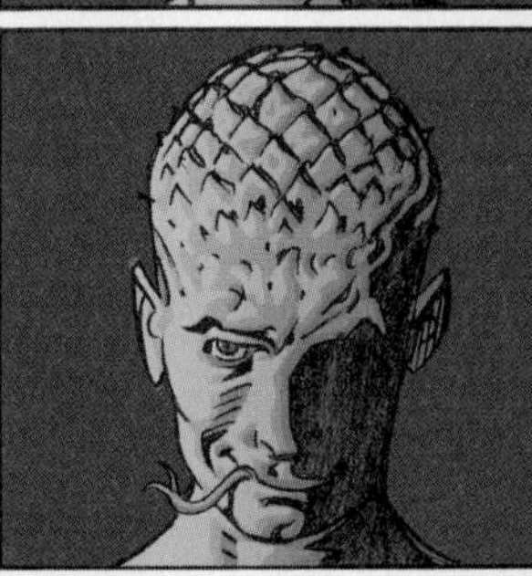

I MUST *GO* NOW, MY SWEETEST.
AYE. YOU *SAID.*
SHALL I VISIT YOU *AGAIN* SOON?

IF IT *PLEASE* YOU, WHY NOT?

WHICH ONE OF THEM IS ***MINE?***

NONE OF THEM.

BUT YOU FATHERED ***THAT*** ONE.

WITH THE GREY EYES AND THE WILD ***HAIR.***

YOUR MOTHER FAVORS A DIFFERENT KIND OF SPORT.
SPEAK NO HARM OF MY MOTHER.
IT IS TRUTH I SPEAK.
THAT HOLE YOU DROPPED FROM IS A COMMON HARBOR FOR ANY--
AHRR!
THAT WAS WELL DONE, LITTLE MONSTER.
I WANTED TO SEE IF YOU HAD YOUR FATHER'S SPIRIT, AND IT SEEMS--
I'LL VISIT YOU AGAIN, ANOTHER DAY. KEEP YOUR DISTANCE FROM THE SONS OF HEAVEN.
AND ENJOY YOUR FEAST.

YOU ARE LILITH.
YES.
I AM IBRIEL, OF THE DOMINIONS. AND MY COMPANION HERE--
I am samael.
called the morningstar.
LILITH, YOU HAVE PEOPLED THIS PLACE WITH THE OFFSPRING OF YOUR LUST. THE STINK OF YOUR OFFENSES REACHES EVEN UNTO HEAVEN.
AND THE HOST OF HEAVEN HAS DECIDED THAT THEY MUST STOP.
AND IF THE HOST DECIDES THAT THE TIDES MUST STOP?
WHAT THEN?
COME OUT OF THE SUN, ANGELS.
I'LL GIVE YOU WATER.
BUT THAT'S ALL I'LL GIVE YOU.

I KNOW YAHWEH KEEPS SILENT ABOUT THE CHOICES I'VE MADE. SO I ASSUME THAT GABRIEL IS MY ACCUSER.
IT MATTERS NOT.
WE SPEAK, AND ACT, AS ONE.
IS THIS SO? I HAD HEARD THAT YOU HAVE A VISION OF YOUR OWN, IBRIEL.
A SILVER CITY, THAT GABRIEL WILL NOT ALLOW YOU TO--
KNOW THIS, LADY. WE ARE EMPOWERED OF THE HOST.
EM-POWERED NOT MERELY TO THREATEN, BUT TO ACT.
AND YET, UNLESS YOU ACT HERE AND NOW--
--TO TELL ME SO IS NO MORE THAN ANOTHER THREAT.
WELL, THE CHOICE LIES WITH YOU. FOR IF YOU DO NOT REPENT YOUR--
WHY DO YOU DO THESE THINGS, LILITH?
YOU WERE MADE FOR ADAM. WHY DO YOU SOIL YOURSELF WITH DEMONS?

WHY? BECAUSE IT PLEASES ME, I SUPPOSE.

I MAY HAVE BEEN MADE FOR ADAM--
--BUT I LIVE FOR MYSELF.

WHICH IS WHAT LIVING MEANS.

WE WILL WITHDRAW, AND LET YOU CONSIDER OUR WORDS.
AT LEAST NOW YOU'RE AWARE THAT HEAVEN STILL WATCHES YOU.

WERE WE NOT SENT TO PUNISH HER? THIS RESOLVES NOTHING.
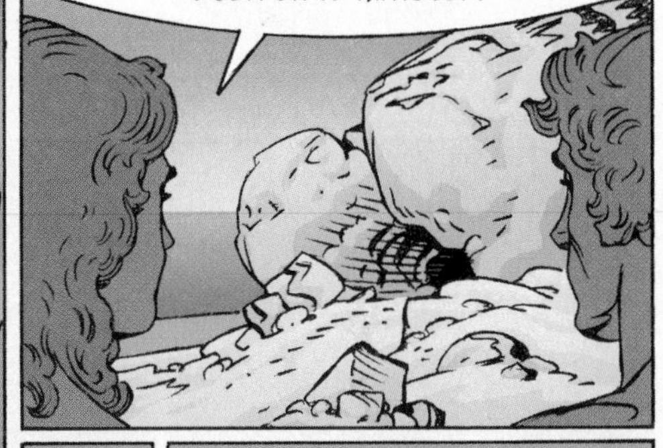
IT RESOLVES MY CURIOSITY. WHICH IS WHY I CAME. IF GABRIEL WANTS A SCOURGING, HE'LL HAVE TO DELIVER IT HIMSELF.

COME AWAY.

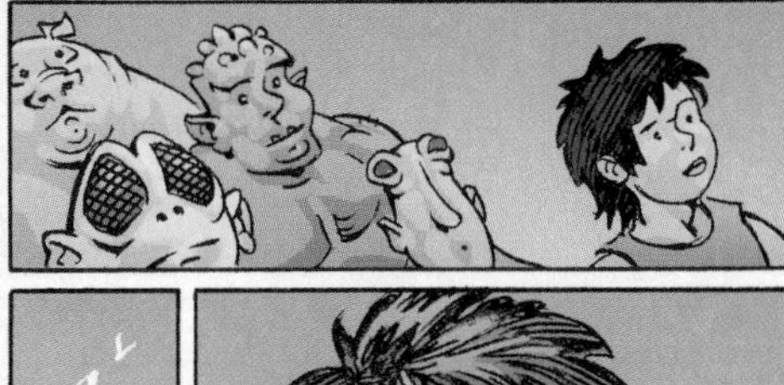

"UNLESS YOU ACT HERE AND *NOW*"?

"WELL, TO THAT THERE WAS BUT *ONE* ANSWER, SURELY."

WHAT, TO PRESERVE OUR SENSE OF OUR OWN DIGNITY BY *KILLING* HER?

I DIDN'T SEE THE *POINT* IN THAT.

SAMAEL, WE *DISCUSSED* THIS IN CONCLAVE. WE REACHED A *DECISION.*

IF SHE CANNOT CONTAIN HER LUSTS, THEN SHE IS TO *DIE.*

BY DOING NOTHING YOU *ERODE* HEAVEN'S AUTHORITY.

HEAVEN'S AUTHORITY DERIVES FROM MY *FATHER.*

AND MY FATHER HAS NOT SPOKEN.

YAHWEH HAS SAID NOTHING TO ANY OF US SINCE THE BUSINESS OF *CREATION* WAS FINISHED.
BUT HE FASHIONED US TO BE HIS HANDS AND HIS *TOOLS.* FOR US TO REMAIN *IDLE* WOULD THEREFORE BE A SIN.
SO WE ARE TO FINISH OUT *ETERNITY* TRYING TO SECOND-GUESS HIS INTENTIONS? TO BE HIS *TOOLS?*
AS IF THERE WERE SOME KIND OF *NOBILITY* IN SELF-ABASEMENT?
AND IS THERE *NOT?*
NONE THAT *I* CAN SEE. WE ARE HIS CHILDREN--HIS FIRST-BORN.
THE FREEDOM *HE* ENJOYS IS *OUR* BIRTHRIGHT TOO.
EVERYTHING DERIVES ITS LIFE FROM HIM. PERHAPS THE *SPARKS* SHOULD SEEK THEIR FREEDOM FROM THE FIRE.
OR MY SHADOW DECLARE AUTONOMY FROM MY *BODY.*
AND LO! WE SWERVE ASIDE *AGAIN,* INTO BARREN RHETORIC.
WHAT IS BARREN IS YOUR *AMBITION,* BROTHER.
I WILL SEEK A *RULING* FROM OUR FATHER ON LILITH.
AND ANOTHER--
--ON *YOU.*

THEY ARE *COMELY,* THE SONS OF HEAVEN.
MOST COMELY.
THEIR HAIR LIKE PRECIOUS *METALS.*
YOUR ANSWERS WERE UNACCEPTABLE.
WE MUST SPEAK *FURTHER.*
LIKE *SILK* THEIR SKIN.
MOST COMELY.
WE HAVE NOT--
--WE HAVE NOT *ESTABLISHED*--
IN FACE, IN FORM, IN FAITH, ALL *PERFECTION.*
AND YET--
--THEY DO NOT *KNOW* THEMSELVES.
NOT UNTIL THEY HAVE KNOWN *ME.*

I HAVE CONSIDERED--
--KILLING MY FATHER.

ASSUMING THAT WAS POSSIBLE, WHAT WOULD IT ACHIEVE?

IT WOULD SET ME FREE.
I WOULD STAND ALONE, THEN.

I THINK IT WOULD DESTROY YOU. YOU'D HAVE HIM HANGING OVER YOUR SHOULDER FOREVER, THEN.
YOU'D NEVER KNOW WHAT YOU MIGHT HAVE BEEN WITHOUT HIS INFLUENCE.

AYE, WELL. THERE'S THE RUB.
HIS INFLUENCE EXTENDS THROUGH EVERYTHING. THERE'S NOWHERE I CAN GO WHERE I WON'T MEET HIM.

THERE'S YOUR OWN SPIRIT, I SUPPOSE.
OR YOUR OWN WILL--

"WHAT-EVER IT IS THAT MAKES YOU HATE HIM."

IT WOULD EXPRESS US. *DEFINE* US.

I SOMETIMES WONDER, GIVEN THAT HE KNOWS WHAT I'M THINKING--
--WHY HE HASN'T DEALT WITH ME ALREADY.

THERE'S NO POINT IN TRYING TO FATHOM HIM, SAMAEL.
NO POINT?

HE'S YOUR MAKER. THAT CAN'T CHANGE. TRY AS YOU MIGHT, YOU CAN NEVER BE YOUR OWN FATHER. YOUR OWN AUTHOR.
THE ONLY VICTORY YOU CAN WIN IS TO BE YOURSELF.

WHAT SELF? A MIND HE MADE FROM WHATEVER MATERIALS HE HAD AT HAND.
THAT RUNS AROUND AND AROUND THE SAME THOUGHTS LIKE A PLANET IN ITS COURSE.
NOT LIKE A PLANET.

"LIKE A STAR--

"--THAT SHINES WITH ITS OWN LIGHT."

I HAVE RUTTED WITH THOUSANDS OF MEN. I HAVE BECOME ADEPT AT GIVING THEM WHAT THEY THINK THEY NEED.

TO SAMAEL, WHOSE PASSION BURNED LIKE THE SUN, I GAVE PLEASURES ABSTRACT AND INTELLECTUAL.

IBRIEL SAW HIMSELF AS ALL SPIRIT. ALL COLD REASON AND LOFTY IMAGINING.

BUT THERE WAS A CORNER IN HIM WARMED BY THE LUST OF THE BODY--

--AND THERE I PITCHED MY TENT.

MY WOMB IS LIKE A GARDEN, WHERE EVERYTHING THAT IS PLANTED COMES TO FRUIT.
I KNEW WHAT WOULD COME OF THIS--

--BUT THEN THE LUST OF THE BODY IS MY JOY AND MY SUSTENANCE.

SOME LITTLE TIME LATER, THE RED SEA WAS WITNESS TO TWO CRIES--
--THE FIRST DEEP, THE SECOND SHRILL.

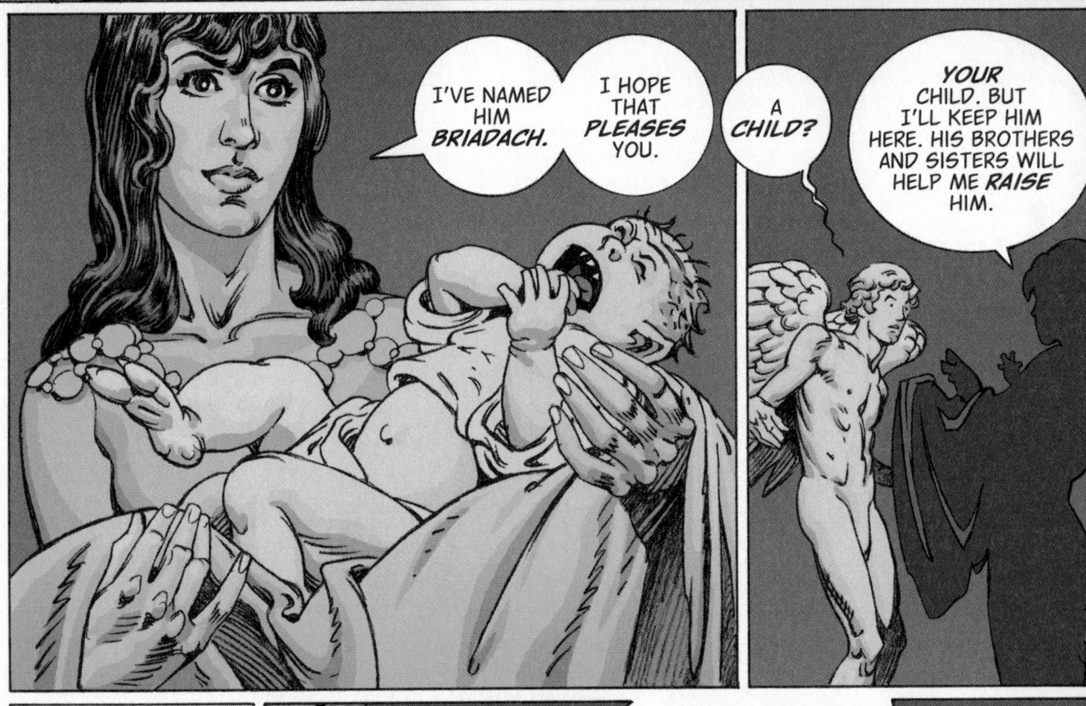
I'VE NAMED HIM BRIADACH.
I HOPE THAT PLEASES YOU.
A CHILD?
YOUR CHILD. BUT I'LL KEEP HIM HERE. HIS BROTHERS AND SISTERS WILL HELP ME RAISE HIM.

HIS BROTHERS AND SISTERS ARE DEMON-SPAWN. HE IS A SIN MADE FLESH.
HOW WILL I BE FORGIVEN FOR THIS? HOW WILL I ATONE?
IBRIEL, HE'S YOUR SON. IF THERE WAS SIN INVOLVED IN HIS MAKING, IT WAS YOURS AND MINE.
NO!
BE SILENT, WOMAN!

YOU!
YOU HAVE EN-TRAPPED ME!
SEDUCED ME!
I NEVER WANTED THIS--

--AND I WILL NOT LET YOU--

I MUST THINK ABOUT THIS. I MUST DECIDE WHAT CAN BE DONE.
I'LL SEE YOU. OR-- OR SEND WORD TO YOU.
IBRIEL!

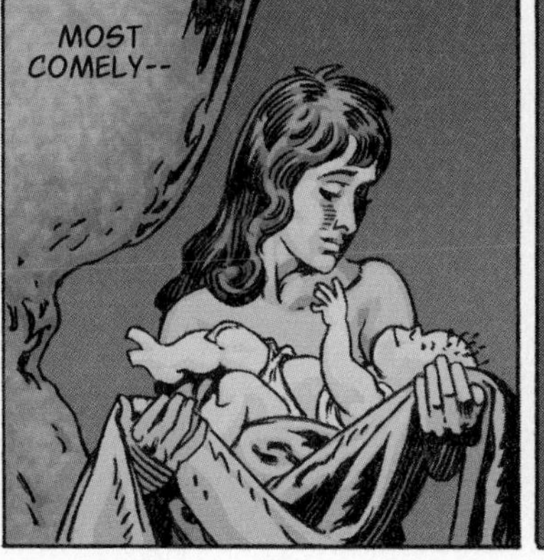
MOST COMELY--

--AND MOST CRUEL.

THE LILIM-- MY CHILDREN-- NUMBER A THOUSAND THOUSAND. SO I HAVE WEPT A THOUSAND THOUSAND TIMES.
BUT FOR THE NUMBERLESS LEGIONS OF THEIR FATHERS, NEVER. NEVER ONCE.
UNTIL NOW.
MOTHER?
MAZIKEEN, NO. NOT NOW. PLEASE--
MOTHER, DON'T CRY.
DON'T GO AWAY FROM US.
I WON'T LET THE ANGEL HURT YOU.
I WON'T LET HIM COME BACK.
WITH HIS STUPID WINGS AND HIS STUPID PICTURES.

"LIKE THE GRAINS OF SAND IN THE DESERT."
"LIKE THE DROPS OF WATER IN THE OCEAN, THAT CANNOT BE COUNTED."
THE LILIM? SHE'D GIVE ME THE LILIM AS A WORK-FORCE?
SO SHE SAID.
BUT WHY?
WHY NOW, WHEN I HAVE GIVEN OVER MY SIN?
IBRIEL, YOU'VE STARED AT YOUR INNER VISIONS TOO LONG. YOU'RE BLIND TO THE WORLD. SHE WANTS TO BUY YOU BACK.
SHE'S MADE HER BID.
SAMAEL-- IS THIS A LESSON, THINK YOU? THAT GOOD CAN BE BROUGHT FORTH FROM EVIL?
IF I WERE GIVEN TO MORALIZING, I'D PROBABLY FIND A DIFFERENT LESSON.
I'LL DO IT.
I'LL BUILD MY SILVER CITY.
IT IS YAHWEH'S WILL, I KNOW IT IS.

"FOR IT IS NOT A CITY, SAMAEL-- IT IS A *SACRAMENT.*

"AN ACT OF *COMMUNION.* YOU UNDERSTAND?"

"YAHWEH WILL COME THERE, AS *BEES* COME TO A WELL-MADE HIVE.

"BUT WHERE BEES BRING ONLY *HONEY,* HE WILL POUR THE CHRYSM OF HIS *GAZE* UPON US ALL.

OFF WITH YOU, RATS!
IF YOU'RE BEHIND ME WHEN I SWING I'LL STAVE YOUR SKULLS IN!

COME ON, BRIADACH. WE'LL CLIMB UP INTO ONE OF THE TOWERS AND LOOK DOWN FROM THERE.
IF AN ANGEL FLIES PAST WE CAN DROP STONES ON HIM.

WHY ARE WE MAKING A CITY FOR THEM, MAZ'KEEN? THEY'RE JUST BIRDS. BIG SILLY BIRDS WITH NOT ENOUGH FEATHERS.

WE'RE BUILDING IT BECAUSE MOTHER SAID SO.
BECAUSE ONE OF THE ANGELS IS HER SPECIAL FRIEND.

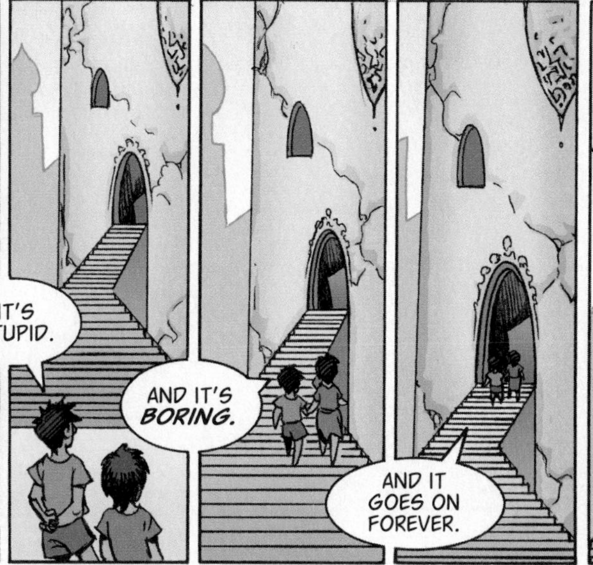

IT'S STUPID.
AND IT'S BORING.
AND IT GOES ON FOREVER.

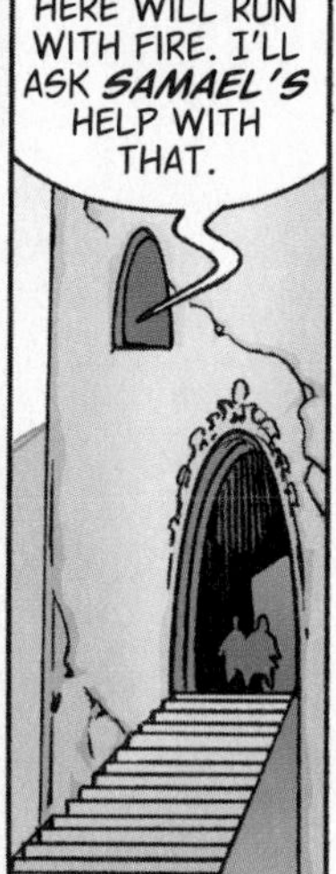

AND THIS FOUNTAIN HERE WILL RUN WITH FIRE. I'LL ASK SAMAEL'S HELP WITH THAT.

AN AMUSING CONCEIT.
NO, IT IS A SYMBOL. THE FIRE IS SPIRIT, FOREVER UPWELLING, FOREVER REBORN.
IBRIEL.
AND IN SOME SENSE IT IS OURSELVES, TOO-- FOR AS FLAME IS, WE ARE ESSENCE WITHOUT SHAPE. ENERGY WITHOUT THE BOUNDS SET BY--

IBRIEL.
LISTEN TO ME.

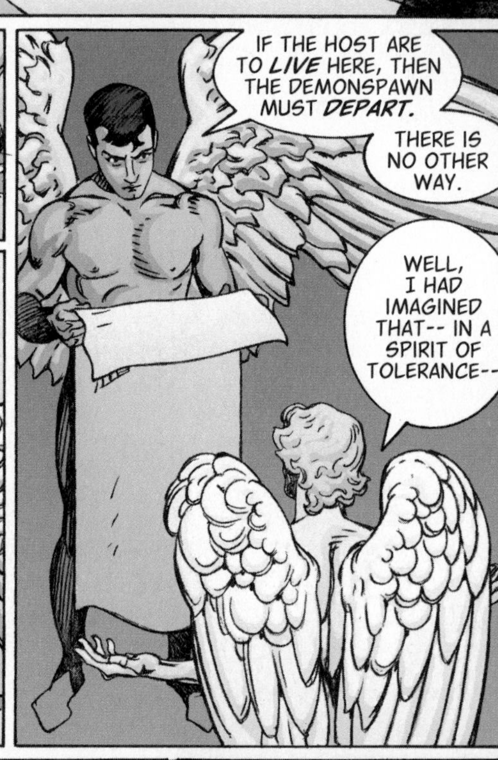
IF THE HOST ARE TO LIVE HERE, THEN THE DEMONSPAWN MUST DEPART.
THERE IS NO OTHER WAY.
WELL, I HAD IMAGINED THAT-- IN A SPIRIT OF TOLERANCE--

AND YOU MUST GIVE HER UP.
OR I WILL PLACE AN INTERDICT ON THIS PLACE, SUCH THAT NO ANGEL WILL EVER ENTER IT.

GABRIEL, I HAVE ALREADY REPENTED OF MY SIN. IT HAS BEEN YEARS SINCE I--
FORGIVE ME. YOU HAVE MERELY FORGONE HER COMPANY A WHILE.
YOU MUST TELL HER THAT HER TOUCH IS LOATHSOME TO YOU. CURSE HER AND CAST HER OFF.
YOUR CITY, IBRIEL. IS IT TO BE A TEMPLE, OR THE PLEASANCE OF A WHORE?
FOR AS GOD IS MY WITNESS, IT CANNOT BE BOTH.
I--
--I WILL CAST HER OFF.
IT IS WELL DONE.
AND I WILL TELL THE HOST THAT THIS SHALL BE THEIR DWELLING PLACE.
THANK YOU, ARCHON.
YOU ARE MOST WELCOME, BROTHER.

A POOL OF FIRE?
A FOUNTAIN OF FIRE, ENDLESSLY UPWELLING.
WHAT SAY YOU, SAMAEL? YOU COULD DO IT WITH A GESTURE.
TO BE BLUNT, IT STRIKES ME AS VULGAR.
IT IS A SYMBOL OF THE SOUL'S ENDLESS RISING.
PLEASE, SAMAEL. THIS IS THE REALIZATION OF MY DREAM.
IF THIS WERE YOUR DREAM, I'D EXPECT HER TO BE IN IT.
BUT I SUPPOSE YOU KNOW YOUR OWN MIND BEST.
SAMAEL, IT WOULD MEAN A GREAT DEAL TO ME.
WELL, I'LL THINK ABOUT IT.
AND I'LL LET YOU KNOW.

MASTER IBRIEL.
CHILD, YOU HAVE NO BUSINESS HERE. YOU MUST--

I TOLD MY MOTHER WHAT YOU SAID. AND SHE SENDS ANSWER.

"IF IBRIEL CAN GOVERN HIS PASSION SO EASILY, HE IS SURELY STRONG ENOUGH TO COMPLETE THE BUILDING OF HIS SILVER HYPOCRISY WITHOUT FURTHER AID FROM ME."

YOU-- YOU TOLD HER WHAT I SAID TO GABRIEL? YOU SPIED ON ME? WHERE IS SHE?
OW!
SHE'S CLOSE BY, BUT SHE WON'T SPEAK TO YOU!
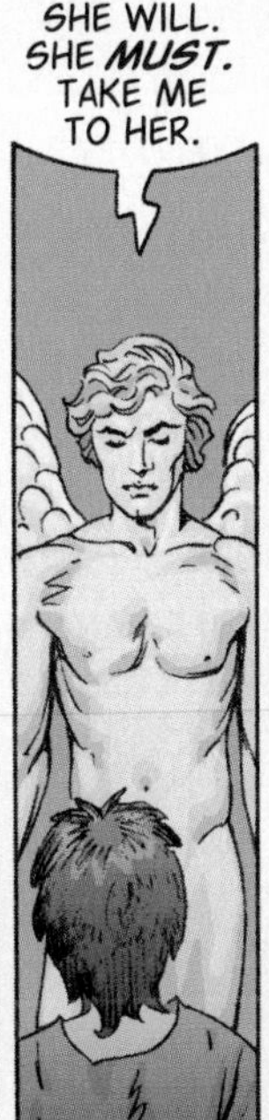
SHE WILL. SHE MUST. TAKE ME TO HER.

SHE CANNOT PULL BACK FROM THIS ENDEAVOR. SHE GAVE HER WORD TO ME.
YOU BROKE YOUR WORD.
THAT IS DIFFERENT.

SHE SWORE AN OATH BEFORE HEAVEN. HEAVEN WILL NOT LET HER RECANT IT.

LEAVE US, GIRL.

I'LL SPEAK WITH HER ALONE.

LILITH? BY CASTING YOU OFF I SHIELD YOU FROM GABRIEL'S WRATH.
BUT IF YOU LEAVE THE CITY UNFINISHED, I SWEAR TO YOU, YOU'VE LOST YOUR LAST FRIEND IN HEAVEN!
YOU UNDERSTAND ME? I CAN'T--
!?

AAAAHH!
MY FATHER'S POISON IS ON THE BLADE.
AND THE BLADE IS IN YOUR HEART.
UHH...
MY SILVER CITY...
MY...
BR... BRIAD...
MY...
MY S...
MY SSSSS...

THEY ARE NOT CHILDREN.
I WILL NOT HEAR THAT WORD USED HERE.
THEY ARE OF TENDER YEARS.
WHICH MAKES THEIR CRIME ALL THE MORE TERRIBLE.
IF THE SEED IS POISONOUS, WHAT WILL WE FIND IN THE FRUIT?
STILL, IT WOULD TROUBLE ME TO VISIT TOO HARSH A PUNISHMENT ON TWO SO YOUNG.
AYE, MICHAEL. AND TO BAPTIZE IBRIEL'S SILVER CITY IN A WELTER OF BLOOD SEEMS A POOR MEMORIAL.
YOUR SCRUPLES DO YOU CREDIT, BROTHERS.
AND I SHARE THEM.
THE CHILDREN OF LILITH WILL BE GIVEN EVERY OPPORTUNITY TO REPENT AND ATONE.
ONLY IF THEY PERSIST IN EVIL--
--WILL THERE BE ANY NEED FOR BLOOD.

SAMAEL.
MICHAEL.
YOU DID NOT JOIN YOUR VOICE WITH OURS IN COUNCIL.

I PREFER TO BE SUR-PRISED.
SO THERE'LL BE AN INAUG-URATION? A CEREMONY OF SOME KIND?
AYE. AND THE FATE OF THE CHILDREN WILL BE DECIDED THEN.

BROTHER, ARE YOU CONTENT TO LIVE LIKE THIS?
WAITING ON OUR FATHER'S WORD, AND WORSHIPPING HIS SILENCE?
I AM... PATIENT.
I BELIEVE HE HAS A PLAN THAT INCLUDES US ALL.
I BELIEVE IT WILL UNFOLD ITSELF IN TIME.

IN TIME?
IN TIME FOR WHAT?

I'M NOT PREPARED TO WAIT.
YOU HAVE NO CHOICE, BROTHER.

OH, WE ALL HAVE A CHOICE.
THE ISSUE-- AS I SEE IT--

--IS WHICH OF US WILL BE PREPARED TO MAKE IT.

I'M *SCARED,* MAZ'KEEN.

OF THE ANGELS? DON'T BE, BRIADACH.

SEE HOW *EASILY* WE KILLED THAT ONE, JUST YOU AND ME?

THEN IMAGINE WHAT *MOTHER* WILL DO, IF THEY TRY TO HURT US.

BUT GOD LOVES THE ANGELS *BETTER* THAN US.

HE'LL MAKE *THEM* WIN.

I WILL HAVE MY CHILDREN.
LADY, I TELL YOU THIS THING CANNOT BE.
DO YOU SEE THIS ARMY AT MY BACK? TELL THEM IT CANNOT BE.
THEY ARE AS NOTHING BESIDE THE HOST OF HEAVEN.
IF THEY ATTACK US, THEY WILL BE SWEPT AWAY LIKE DUST.
THIS DUST IS ARMED.
THIS DUST IS A NATION--
--AND YOU WILL NEVER TAME OR QUELL IT.
YOU MUST WAIT UPON JUS-TICE.
OH SO MUST YOU, ANGEL, SO MUST YOU ALL.
I'LL GIVE YOU ONE TURN OF THE GLASS.
THEN, IF MY CHILDREN ARE NOT RETURNED TO ME--
--WE WILL TAKE BACK WHAT WE MADE.

ANGELS! SONS OF YAHWEH! THIS IS A ***SOLEMN*** MOMENT.

YOU LOOK AROUND YOU AND ARE JOYOUS AT THE GIFT OUR DEAD BROTHER HAS BEQUEATHED TO YOU. THIS CITY ALL OF ***SILVER.***

REPENT OF YOUR SIN, MAZIKEEN, DAUGHTER OF LILITH. ABASE YOURSELVES BEFORE HEAVEN'S JUDGMENT SEAT.
BEG FOR THE PARDON OF THOSE YOU'VE WRONGED.
STUPID, HORRIBLE ANGEL.
I'M GLAD HE'S DEAD.
I'LL BE GLAD WHEN YOU'RE DEAD.
SO WILL I!
AND HOW CAN MERCY REACH OUT TO THOSE WHO REFUSE ITS EMBRACE?
HOW CAN MERCY FIND THOSE WHO STRIVE SO HARD TO HIDE FROM IT?
IT WRINGS MY HEART TO TAINT OUR SOLEMN JOY WITH DARKER EMOTION.
BUT WE HAVE TAKEN STRONG POISON.
NOW WE MUST TAKE STRONG MEDICINE.
?
HE WISHED THE FOUNTAIN TO RUN WITH FLAME.

IS THIS FLAME **ENOUGH**, BROTHER?

...OR DO YOU THINK HE WAS AIMING FOR A MORE **EXTREME** STATE-MENT?

LUCIFER, YOU MAY NOT INTERFERE HERE. THE VOICE OF HEAVEN HAS SPOKEN.
no.
THE VOICE I HEAR IS YOURS, GABRIEL.
JUST AS THE SIN IS YOURS.
FOR YOUR VIRTUE IS NOT CONTENT UNLESS IT CAN INTIMIDATE AND ENSLAVE THE VIRTUE OF OTHERS.
WOULD YOU CHALLENGE ME BEFORE THE ENTIRE HOST?
CHALLENGE YOU? YOU'RE LIKE A DROP OF DEW ON A LEAF, BROTHER.
AND LOOK, THE SUN IS RISING, AND YOU CANNOT STOP IT.

ALL THE SUNS OF ALL THE WORLDS, IN FACT. SET THE CHILDREN FREE--
--OR THOSE SUNS WILL DANCE IN THIS FOUNTAIN, AND THE ASHES OF YOUR HOLINESS WILL MIX WITH THE ASHES OF YOUR CITY.
YOU CARE NOTHING FOR THE CHILDREN. YOU'RE JUST LOOKING FOR AN EXCUSE TO DEFY ME.
I CARE FOR TRUTH. MY OWN TRUTH.
GOD IS MY TRUTH.
AND NOW GOD WILL JUDGE BETWEEN US.
NO.

MICHAEL, STAND BESIDE ME AND HELP ME TO END THIS.
I DO NOT WISH TO SEE DIVISION AMONG THE HOST, GABRIEL.
AND SO I HAVE KEPT SILENT.
I AM TO BLAME IN THIS.
FOR THEIR CRIME OF MURDER, IT IS MEET THAT THE CHILDREN OF LILITH SHOULD BE EXILED FROM THIS PLACE.
WE DON'T CARE.
WE DON'T EVEN WANT TO STAY IN YOUR FILTHY CITY.
THEN LEAVE IT.
PERHAPS MY BROTHER SAMAEL WILL ESCORT YOU TO THE GATE.
!
THIS IS A TRAVESTY OF JUSTICE.
JUSTICE IS MY FATHER'S PREROGATIVE.
THE REST OF US...
THE REST OF US CAN ONLY DO WHAT WE THINK IS RIGHT.

ANGELS OF THE HOST! I RENOUNCE MY NAME AND MY BIRTHRIGHT. I AM SAMAEL NO LONGER.
NOW I AM ONLY WHAT I WAS MADE TO BE--THE LUCIFER. THE BEARER OF THE LIGHT AND THE FIRE.

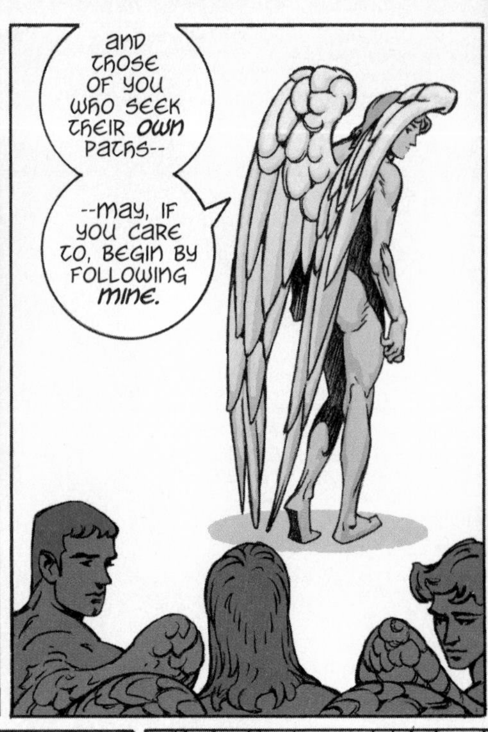
AND THOSE OF YOU WHO SEEK THEIR OWN PATHS--
--MAY, IF YOU CARE TO, BEGIN BY FOLLOWING MINE.

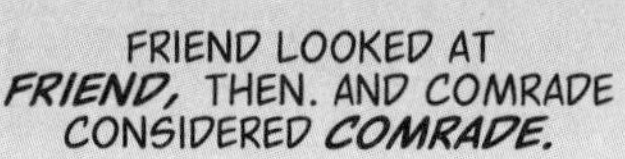
FRIEND LOOKED AT FRIEND, THEN. AND COMRADE CONSIDERED COMRADE.

A SILENCE FELL ACROSS THE PLAZA, SUDDEN AND HEAVY.

AS HE WALKED TOWARD THE GATE, THEY BEGAN TO FALL IN BEHIND HIM.
HE DIDN'T LOOK BACK.

HE DIDN'T SEEM TO CARE.

MOTHER!
THE LUCIFER SAVED US!
WITH FIRE!
SO NOW YOU'RE A PLANET THAT'S LEFT ITS ORBIT.
no.
as you said, I'm a star. I'll borrow light from no one.
until we meet again, Lilith.
HE LEFT ME, THEN. AND THE REBELS FOLLOWED HIM.
FOR A STAR DRAWS MANY THINGS IN ITS WAKE, WHETHER IT WILL OR NO.

--UNTIL WE *FLOWER.*

END

To: Lucifer Morningstar
From: Gaudium of the Seventeenth Harmony (well, ex)

Hi.
I mean, greetings.
Being as how your ~~squeeze~~ Lieutenant, Mazikeen, daughter of Lilith, has gone awol, the team felt that I should give you the final score. Which was that we won.

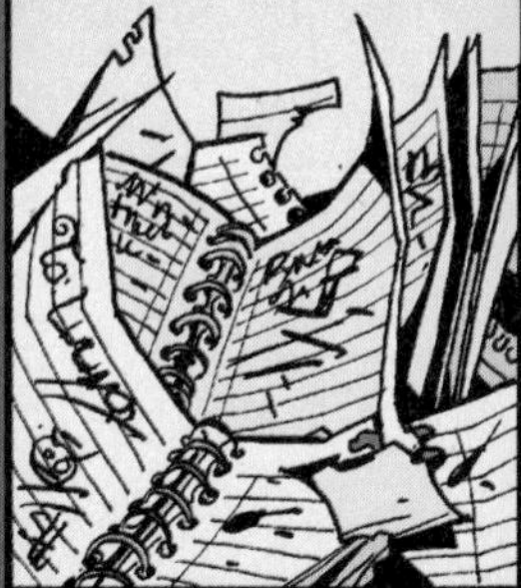
We cleared out all the immortals from your universe with a couple of days to spare, so we awarded ourselves a holiday with the centaurs of River Holt.

And a ~~wild time~~ much needed rest was had by all.
HORSE

Seriously, though, Maz was right there with us until the bottom of the ninth. Then she took off and disappeared, with some talk about there being one last immortal who'd somehow got under our radar. The kera theodmet? Something like that.

Anyway, Elaine says we're good, but maybe you want to check in with her at some point and get the skinny on that one.

Then I come back and everyone's yammering on about God's name. I said "his name's Yahweh, there's no big mystery." But they're like, "no, no, no! Now that God's up and left us, his name is fading from the face of creation and then creation itself will shrivel up like some kind of salted slug and we're all gonna die..."

Well, whatever. I just do my job.

With respects and salutations and a tactful reminder that we haven't any of us been paid for this gig, I remain,

Your damned ex-cherub

Gaudium

I USED THE BALLPEEN HAMMER BECAUSE THE PAIN GETS TRAPPED BETWEEN THE WALLS.
IT COMES FROM A WORLD WHERE EVERYTHING IS AS HEAVY AS LEAD. FORTUNATELY, I SPEAK THAT LANGUAGE.
THERE WAS A SOUND THAT WAS LIKE "YOUR MEDICATION!" FIVE SOUNDS, REALLY.
AND THEY HAD SARAH'S VOICE.
THAT MADE ME DEPRESSED AFTER A WHILE. IN THE WORLD BETWEEN THE WALLS, I DON'T SEE SARAH THAT MUCH.
I WAS MISSING HER. I WAS WONDERING WHEN THIS WORLD WOULD END AND THE OTHER WORLD WOULD START AGAIN.
I ASKED THE MEN WHO CAME. ONE OF THEM SAID "JESUS CHRIST"--
--AND THREW UP SICK THAT SMELLED OF ORANGES.
AND I THOUGHT SARAH'S NOT GONNA LIKE THAT.
AND I THOUGHT IT'S TOO LATE NOW. (TOO LATE FOR WHAT, I WONDER?)
AND I THOUGHT I REALLY SHOULD'VE GONE BACK TO THE DOCTOR--
029684 265 1478
CHARLES W. GILMOUR
TAKE ONE TABLET
FOUR TIMES DAILY
Risperidone 1mg
NO REFILLS
--WHEN THE BOTTLE DIDN'T RATTLE ANYMORE.

CALIFORNIA.
FZZZT
FZZZT
CLICK
CURLY? WHASSAMATTER?
WHAT'RE YOU DOING WAY OVER *THERE?*
GO BACK TO *SLEEP,* JILL.
IT'S JUST A *THOUGHT* THAT WILL NOT LET ME REST.
NO MORE THAN THAT.
THERE'S *OTHER* THINGS WE COULD DO BESIDES SLEEP, Y'KNOW?
I MEAN, IF YOU'RE *RESTLESS.*
I CONFESS I AM-- UNEASY.
SOMEONE IS *COMING.*
SOMEONE WE WILL NOT BE *HAPPY* TO SEE.

SHIT! YOU MEAN THE BITCH WITH HALF A *FACE?* MAZIKEEN?
IS SHE *FINALLY* GOING TO MAKE HER MOVE?
NO.

THIS FEAR HAS A DIFFERENT *TEXTURE* TO IT. COARSER. OLDER.

SOMEONE I KNEW LONG *AGO,* PERHAPS.

WELL, SINCE WE'RE BOTH UP-- AND SINCE FUCKING YOUR *BRAINS* OUT DOESN'T SEEM TO BE AN OPTION--

--I'LL GO FIX US SOME *COFFEE.*

COME *IN,* WOMAN.

YOU'RE LATE, AND LOOKED FOR.
THERE'S NAUGHT ON YOUR TABLE SAVE THIS SAD OFFERING THAT WE BROUGHT OURSELVES.
THE WOLF BENEATH THE TREE
PART 1 OF 4
MIKE CAREY Writer
PETER GROSS & RYAN KELLY Artists
JARED K. FLETCHER- Lettering DANIEL VOZZO- Colors and Separations
CHRISTOPHER MOELLER- Cover Painter MARIAH HUEHNER- Editor
Based on characters created by GAIMAN, KIETH and DRINGENBERG

AUSTIN. THE U.S. DISTRICT COURT FOR WEST TEXAS.
JUNE 12TH. 10.30AM.
YOUR HONOR, I OBJECT.
MY CLIENT'S ANSWER SHOWS YET AGAIN THAT HE'S NOT FIT TO PLEAD.
COUNSELLOR--
THAT IN FACT HE DOESN'T EVEN UNDERSTAND WHAT HE'S BEING ACCUSED OF.
COUNSELLOR, YOUR PRE-TRIAL SUBMISSIONS WERE HEARD AND PRONOUNCED ON.
PLEASE DON'T RAISE THEM AGAIN AT THIS POINT. MISTER GILMOUR, YOU WILL ANSWER THE QUESTION.
I DON'T THINK I GET THE QUESTION. I NEVER ACTUALLY MET GOD.
YET YOU TOLD DETECTIVE KRUEGER THAT GOD GIVES YOU MISSIONS TO CARRY OUT--
I NEVER MET HIM. NOT FACE TO FACE.
--AND THAT HE MADE YOU PICK UP THAT HAMMER.
ARE YOU NOW SAYING THAT YOU WERE SOMEHOW MISQUOTED?

GOD SOMETIMES ***MOVES*** ME-- KIND OF-- INTO ANOTHER ***WORLD.***
WHERE THERE'S SOMETHING HE WANTS ***DONE.***
I ALWAYS TELL ***SARAH*** BEFORE I GO. IN FACT, I'VE BEEN-- I'VE BEEN LOOKING FOR HER BECAUSE--

YOUR WIFE IS ***DEAD,*** MISTER GILMOUR.
NO SIR. SHE'S ***OUT*** RIGHT NOW.
YOU ***MURDERED*** HER. WITH SEVENTEEN ***BLOWS*** FROM A BALLPEEN HAMMER.

AND YOUR SON, ROBERT-- HE WAS STILL ***ALIVE*** AT THIS POINT.
BOBBY. HIS NAME IS BOBBY.
HE HAD TO SIT THERE AND ***WATCH,*** KNOWING HE WAS GOING TO BE NEXT.

"--YOU HAVE PLACED YOURSELF FAR OUTSIDE THE SCOPE OF ITS MERCY."
AND WHAT ELSE DID MY BROTHER SAY?
BE FRANK, URIEL. NO WORDS OF LUCIFER'S CAN MOVE ME TO ANGER.
HE SAID, MICHAEL, THAT AS LONG AS THIS THRONE REMAINS EMPTY, CREATION WILL CONTINUE TO DISINTEGRATE.
HE SAID NOTHING WOULD SURVIVE. AT LEAST--
--NOTHING OF YAHWEH'S.NOTHING MY FATHER MADE. MY OWN CREATION WON'T BE TOUCHED.
I'LL KEEP THE BORDER OPEN FOR AS LONG AS I CAN--BUT ONLY TO MORTALS, OF COURSE.
THE REST OF YOU WILL HAVE TO GET BY AS BEST YOU CAN.

AS IF HEAVEN'S HOST WOULD WAIT ON LUCIFER'S CHARITY.
ARE THERE OTHER PATHS OPEN TO US, MICHAEL? IT SEEMED FROM WHAT HE SAID--
THERE ARE OTHER PATHS.

SO MY FATHER HAS ABANDONED US TO OUR FATE. AND BY DOING SO, HAS DOOMED US.
STILL, WE ARE WHAT HE MADE US, URIEL.

HIS OWN MOST PERFECT ECHOES.
HIS OWN MOST PERSISTENT AFTERIMAGES.

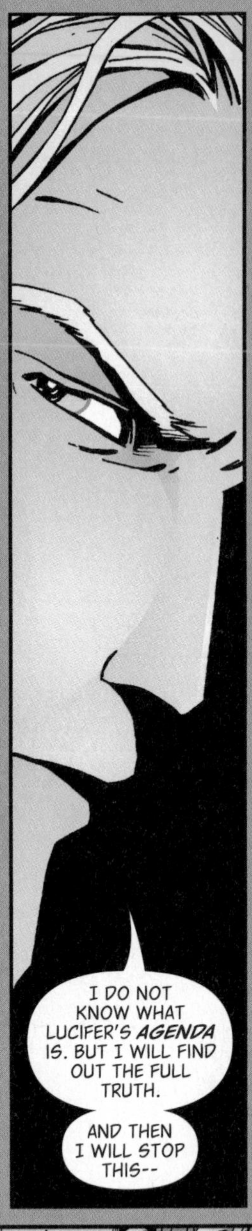
I DO NOT KNOW WHAT LUCIFER'S AGENDA IS. BUT I WILL FIND OUT THE FULL TRUTH.
AND THEN I WILL STOP THIS--

--NO MATTER WHAT THE COST.

THIS PLACE IS RENTED, YOU SONS OF BITCHES!
I'M GONNA GIVE YOU A SLOW COUNT OF TEN--
--THEN IF I CAN STILL SEE YOU, I'M GONNA CUT YOU INTO DECORATIVE FUCKING PASTRY SHAPES.
SO. MY OPTIONS ARE TO PUT OUT YOUR EYES--
--TO PUT OUT THE SUN--
--OR TO DISARM YOU.
AAAAA!
NOW. I SEE YOU'VE JUST THE ONE HAND, WOMAN.
IF YOU WANT TO KEEP IT, CALL BERGELMIR TO ME. I'D HAVE WORDS WITH HIM.
I'M ALREADY HERE, FENRIS.
AH! MY COUSIN BERGELMIR.
THESE ARE MY FRIENDS, ABONSAM AND BET JO'GIE--

BE *MERCIFUL* TO THE WOMAN, FOR SHE DOES NOT *KNOW* YOU.

AND I HAVE BEEN YOUR *FRIEND,* EREWHILE, IN OTHER TIMES AND PLACES.

AND AM I NOT *BLESSED* IN SUCH FRIENDS? SO TRUE. SO STEADFAST.

SO *BRAVE.*

WATCH HIM *CLOSE,* FENRIS. SEE! HE WEAVES A RUNE.

BUT BERGELMIR KNOWS THAT EVEN *MAGICS* BREAK WHEN THEY TOUCH ME. HE'D NEVER BE SO FOOLISH.

IT WAS A *CALMING,* NOTHING MORE.

I WANT NO VIOLENCE HERE.

AFTER THEY PASSED *JUDGMENT* ON THE HAMMER, THEY TOOK ME TO A PLACE WHERE THEY THOUGHT IT COULDN'T *FIND* ME.

THEY TOOK ME BETWEEN THE *WALLS.*

MY NAME IS CHARLIE GILMOUR.

MY DOSAGE IS 5 MILLIGRAMS OF *CLOZAPINE* FOUR TIMES A DAY AND 10 MILLIGRAMS OF *VALPROATE* THREE TIMES A DAY.

THAT'S JUST *HERE,* THOUGH.

IN THE *REAL* WORLD, I'M ON RISPERIDONE.

SURE, CHARLIE. JUST TAKE THE FUCKING *PILLS,* OKAY?

ONE AT A TIME. I HAVE TO TICK YOU *OFF.*

WE HAVE TO TAKE THE *PILLS* ONE AT A TIME HERE. WE HAVE TO *TICK.*

THE CAMERAS *SQUEAK* A LITTLE AS THEY MOVE. HIGH UP ON THE WALL WHERE WE CAN'T *REACH.*

AND *BETWEEN* THE WALLS--

--IT'S ALL *QUIET* NOW.

QUIET STRETCHING FURTHER AND FURTHER. MADE OF *LEAD.*

ALL THINGS MOVE TOWARDS THEIR *END,* BERGELMIR.
WOULDN'T YOU *SAY?*
I'VE ALWAYS SEEN THINGS MORE IN TERMS OF *CYCLES.*
YOU KNOW-- GROWTH, DECAY, GROWTH. THE BIG *DANCE* THAT GOES ON AND ON FOREVER.
YOU *MISTAKE* ME.
I WASN'T INDULGING IN COSMIC *PLATITUDES.*
HERE. NOW. THINGS MOVE TO A CLOSE. THE HOUR OF THE *WOLF* IS COME AT LAST.
SOME WILL TRY TO *STOP* IT.
THEY MUST FALL. THEY MUST *PERISH.* I MUST BE STRONG ENOUGH TO RIP OUT ANGELS *HEARTS,* FOR ANGELS WILL STAND AGAINST ME. ANGELS AND HALF-ANGELS.
YOU *WANT* SOMETHING FROM ME, FENRIS.
ONLY WHAT'S MINE ALREADY.
INFORMATION THAT I *GAVE* TO YOU.
KNOWING HOW *GOOD* YOU ARE AT SURVIVAL. KNOWING I'D NEED IT ONE DAY.

NINE HUNDRED YEARS AGO, I HOSTED A BANQUET.
FOR FORMER ENEMIES, MOSTLY. TO PROVE I BORE NO GRUDGES AGAINST THEM.
AYE, I REMEMBER THAT DAY.
AH, BUT I DON'T. I AM FENRIS, THE WOLF WHO DEVOURS, AND NOTHING ESCAPES MY TOUCH.
WHEN THERE IS NAUGHT ELSE TO DESTROY, I NEEDS MUST TURN ON MYSELF.
THAT OFFAL ON THE TABLE-- I THOUGHT THAT HE WAS ONE OF THEM, BUT I WAS WRONG.
TELL ME THEIR NAMES. THE ONES WHO ATE MY BREAD AND MY MEAT. AND I WILL LET YOUR WOMAN LIVE, SO YOU MAY HAVE THE USE OF HER UNTIL THE WORLDS FALL.
HE HAS THE NAMES.
HE SIGNS FOR US TO GO.
YEAH. SURE. IN A MINUTE.

IT'S *ALIVE,* ISN'T IT? LIVING SILVER.

WHEN YOU'RE *FUCKING* HIM, DOES HE EVER MAKE YOU--?

TAKE YOUR *PAWS* OFF ME!

GO GET YOUR CREEPY KICKS SOMEWHERE *ELSE!*

UFFFF!

BET JO'GIE. FIND SOME *FITTER* TIME FOR THIS. WE HAVE TO GO AND CHECK OUR *OTHER* CHARGE.

YOU WERE *PREGNANT* A WHILE BACK, WEREN'T YOU, SWEETMEAT?

AND YOU GOT *RID* OF IT.

WELL, GOOD JOB. COPULATION'S ABOUT *YOU,* NOT THE NEXT FUCKING GENERATION.

SPIKE THEM IN THE *WOMB,* OR STRANGLE THEM IN THE *COT.* IT'S ALL THE SAME.

EXCEPT IT WAS *TWINS.* AND YOU ONLY GOT THE *ONE* OF THEM.

ENJOY.

DESTINY'S GARDEN.
IF I TRY TO REACH YOUR DOOR BY WALKING THESE *PATHS,* I WILL BE HERE A LONG WHILE.
TIME *PRESSES.* I ASK RESPECTFULLY--
ENTER, MICHAEL DEMIURGOS.
YOU ARE **WELCOME** HERE.

AND INEVITABLE, DESTINY OF THE ENDLESS?
AS ALL THINGS ARE.
YOUR COMING HERE AT THIS TIME IS WITHIN THE SCHEME OF THINGS. THE SCHEME OF THINGS IS KNOWN.
THAT IS WHY I AM HERE. AS YOU NO DOUBT ALREADY KNOW.
YOU WISH TO READ AHEAD IN THE BOOK, MICHAEL DEMIURGUS. I MUST REFUSE YOU THAT. BUT FEAR NOT. YOUR JOURNEY WILL NOT BE WASTED.
NOT WASTED? I DO NOT SEE--
BY SOMETHING I SAY TO YOU, I WILL ACCIDENTALLY CONVEY MORE INFORMATION THAN I INTENDED.
PLEASE. MY OTHER GUESTS ARE BEGINNING TO SEE SINISTER IMPLICATIONS IN MY ABSENCE.

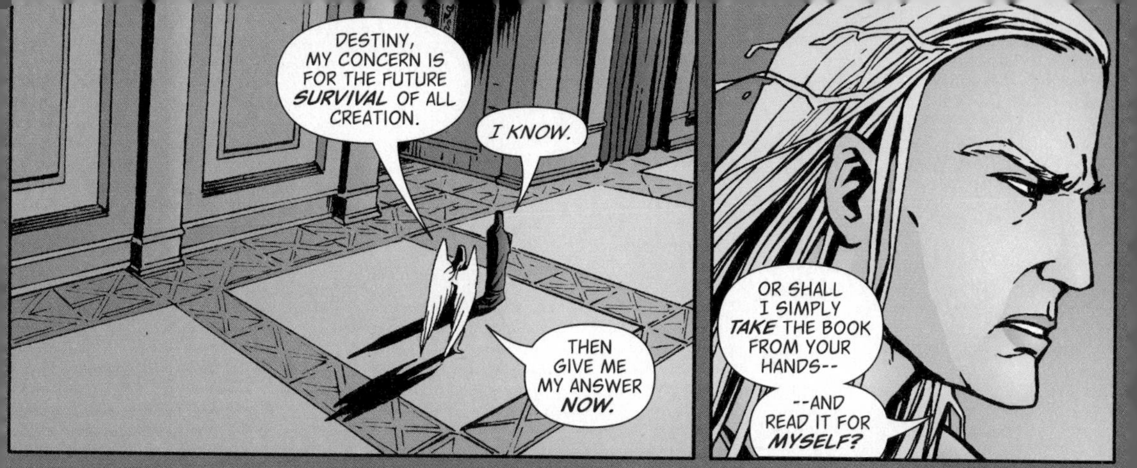
DESTINY, MY CONCERN IS FOR THE FUTURE SURVIVAL OF ALL CREATION.
I KNOW.
THEN GIVE ME MY ANSWER NOW.
OR SHALL I SIMPLY TAKE THE BOOK FROM YOUR HANDS--
--AND READ IT FOR MYSELF?

THE BOOK HAS NO EXISTENCE SEPARATE FROM ME. AND SO YOU DO NOT DO THIS.
THE GLASS WILL TURN TWICE, AND THEN I WILL COMMIT THE INDISCRETION I SPOKE OF.

IN THE MEANTIME, SIT. ENJOY THE HOSPITALITY OF MY HOUSE.
THOUGH THE CIRCUMSTANCES ARE STRAINED, THERE MAY STILL BE SOME PLEASURE TO BE HAD--

--FROM A FAMILY REUNION.
HELLO, DAD.
HOW ARE THINGS WITH YOU?

LUCIFER.
MICHAEL.
YOUR PRESENCE HERE IS NOT **WELCOME.**

YOU HAVE ALREADY **STATED** YOUR POSITION. YOU WILL STAND IN YOUR GATEWAY AND **WATCH** US FALL.
SO CLEARLY YOU HAVE NO **INTEREST** IN POSSIBLE SOLUTIONS.

IS THAT WHY **YOU'RE** HERE? TO LOOK FOR **ANSWERS?**
OF COURSE. AND I WILL NOT BE STAYED OR **DEFLECTED** BY YOU!

"NO VISITATION OF CONSCIENCE."
SO.
CHARLIE.
"NO PROMPTING OF PITY."
HOW DO YOU FEEL YOUR FIRST DAY WITH US HAS GONE?
HAVE YOU FOUND YOUR FEET YET?
THERE ARE ECHOES HERE.
I'M WAITING FOR SOME-ONE.
BUT NONE OF THEM HAVE FACES.
WHAT? A VISITOR?
BUT YOU DON'T HAVE ANY LIVING RELATIVES, DO YOU?
NOT IN THIS WORLD.
IN THE OTHER WORLD I'VE GOT SARAH. AND MY SON, BOBBY.
WELL, IT'S GOOD THAT YOU'RE COMING TO TERMS WITH THEIR DEATHS.
I'LL SEE YOU FOR A FULL SESSION TOMORROW. YOU CAN TAKE HIM STRAIGHT TO HIS CELL, DON.
YES, DOCTOR SPEARS.

I READ ABOUT YOU, GILMOUR. ABOUT HOW YOU KILLED YOUR KID AND ALL.
LOST MY OWN KID ABOUT A YEAR AGO. LEUKEMIA. YOU STEP OUT OF LINE, I'LL BREAK YOU AND LAUGH WHILE I'M DOING IT.
THE MAN WITH THE FEATHERS. IS HE--?
FEATHERS. RIGHT.
DON'T PISS ME OFF.
ONE SECURE. TWELVE-OH-TWO.
SLEEP TIGHT, GILMOUR.
RATCH-TCHK

THE AIR-- THE AIR WAS SO STILL I THOUGHT I'D WALKED INTO A CATHEDRAL. AS THOUGH THERE WAS A CEILING SO HIGH UP I COULDN'T SEE IT.
AS THOUGH SOMEONE WAS ABOUT TO CLEAR HIS THROAT AND START IN ON A SERMON.
IT'S FUNNY.
TO GET OUT FROM BETWEEN THE WALLS-- TO SEE SARAH AND BOBBY AGAIN--
--I SHOULD'VE BEEN SO HAPPY.
BUT IT FELT LIKE THE END OF THE WORLD.

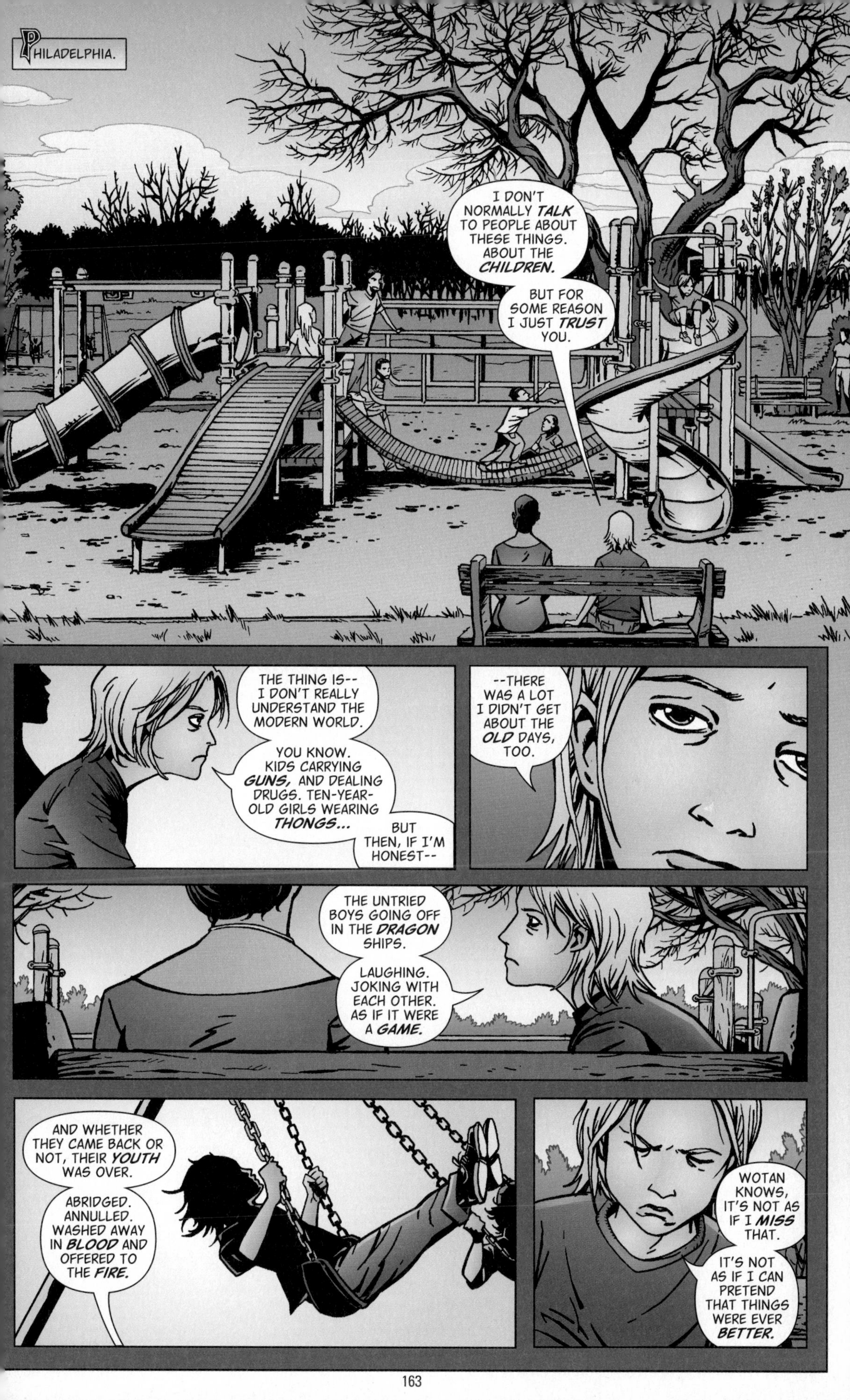
PHILADELPHIA.
I DON'T NORMALLY *TALK* TO PEOPLE ABOUT THESE THINGS. ABOUT THE *CHILDREN.*
BUT FOR SOME REASON I JUST *TRUST* YOU.
THE THING IS-- I DON'T REALLY UNDERSTAND THE MODERN WORLD.
YOU KNOW. KIDS CARRYING *GUNS,* AND DEALING DRUGS. TEN-YEAR-OLD GIRLS WEARING *THONGS...*
BUT THEN, IF I'M HONEST--
--THERE WAS A LOT I DIDN'T GET ABOUT THE *OLD* DAYS, TOO.
THE UNTRIED BOYS GOING OFF IN THE *DRAGON* SHIPS.
LAUGHING. JOKING WITH EACH OTHER. AS IF IT WERE A *GAME.*
AND WHETHER THEY CAME BACK OR NOT, THEIR *YOUTH* WAS OVER.
ABRIDGED. ANNULLED. WASHED AWAY IN *BLOOD* AND OFFERED TO THE *FIRE.*
WOTAN KNOWS, IT'S NOT AS IF I *MISS* THAT.
IT'S NOT AS IF I CAN PRETEND THAT THINGS WERE EVER *BETTER.*

WHAT ABOUT YOU. ARE YOU STAYING HERE LONG?
NO. JUST FOR TODAY,
I'M THE BAIT, IDUN. AND THE COVER, TOO.
I FILL YOUR EYES AND FOX YOUR SENSES SO THAT FENRIS CAN GET IN CLOSE.
FENRIS? FENRIS THE--
AAAAHH!
YES. HIM.
THE WOLF.
YOU'RE A GOD OF YOUTH, IDUN.
TO BE HONEST, YOU WERE GETING A BIT OLD FOR THE JOB ANYWAY.
FENRIS. HAH!
THEN THE WOMAN HAS BEGUILED ME TO MY DEATH.
THAT'S WHAT BET JO'GIE DOES.

AND THIS IS WHAT I DO.
BUT I THOUGHT OUR DIFFERENCES SETTLED.
I ATE AT YOUR TABLE!
THE WOLF BENEATH THE TREE
PART 2 OF 4
MIKE CAREY Writer
PETER GROSS & RYAN KELLY Artists
JARED K. FLETCHER- Lettering DANIEL VOZZO- Colors and Separations
CHRISTOPHER MOELLER- Cover Painter MARIAH HUEHNER- Editor
Based on characters created by GAIMAN, KIETH and DRINGENBERG

TEXAS.
GOD HAS SHOWN ME THE WAY AGAIN.
BUT I DON'T KNOW WHAT HE MEANT.
THE WALLS FELL DOWN AND THE EARTH AND THE SKY OPENED UP.
AND SARAH AND BOBBY WERE THERE BENEATH THE TREE, WAITING FOR ME.
I-- I'VE BEEN SO MIXED UP SINCE THEY CHANGED MY MEDS.
I'VE BEEN MISSING HER REAL BAD. I'M SCARED SOMETHING'S HAPPENED TO HER.
HEY, CHARLIE-- YOU'RE BLOCKING THE FUCKIN' TV.
SHUT UP!
SHUT UP SHUT UP SHUT UP!

SO WHAT DO *YOU* THINK, DOCTOR SPEARS?

IS GILMOUR *ADJUSTING?*

I'D HAVE TO SAY *NO,* BURCH.

IT'S STRANGE. IF ANYTHING HIS DELUSIONAL SYSTEM IS GETTING *MORE* ENTRENCHED.

HE'S NOT RESPONDING TO THE *CLOZAPINE.* HE MIGHT AS WELL BE POPPING M&MS.

HE HAS CONVULSIVE FITS, HEARS AT LEAST *SEVEN* DISTINCT VOICES INCLUDING GOD'S, AND GOES ON DELUSIONAL *QUESTS.*

WELL WE'RE NOT A HOSPITAL. THERE'S ALWAYS *SOLITARY.*

QUESTS FOR *WHAT,* EXACTLY?

THE HOUSE OF DESTINY OF THE ENDLESS.
NOW.

INVITED? YOU WERE SUMMONED HERE?
I DO NOT UNDER- STAND.
IS IT THAT SLIPPERY A CONCEPT, MICHAEL?

DESTINY TOLD ME THAT SOMEONE HERE WOULD NEED MY HELP.
AND I'M ASSURED I'LL LEARN SOMETHING TO MY ADVANTAGE.
SO-- MUCH AGAINST MY BETTER JUDGMENT-- HERE I AM.

BUT DESPITE THE URGENCY OF MY MISSION-- THE MAGNITUDE OF WHAT IS AT STAKE--
--NO INVITATION WAS ISSUED TO ME.

YOU WERE ALREADY COMING. IT WOULD HAVE SERVED NO PURPOSE.
PLEASE. SIT AND EAT.

I DID NOT COME HERE TO BE FED OR ENTERTAINED. I CAME TO SEE WHETHER OR NOT CREATION COULD BE SAVED.
AND I FIND YOUR ANTICIPATION OF HOW I WILL ACT PRESUMPTUOUS.
I SYMPATHIZE, IT IS HARD TO TAKE.
I REGRET ANY OFFENSE, MICHAEL. I CAN ONLY REPEAT THAT YOU WILL HAVE YOUR ANSWER SOON.
IN THE MEANTIME--
ENOUGH! I WILL SIT, AND BIDE MY TIME.
DESTINY, HOW WOULD YOU FEEL ABOUT A SMALL WAGER?
BEFORE THIS MEAL IS OVER, I'LL DO SOMETHING THAT ISN'T WRITTEN IN YOUR BOOK.
ALL THINGS ARE WRITTEN THERE. THE WAGER WOULD BE MEANINGLESS.
BUT JUST FOR THE HELL OF IT-- SO TO SPEAK.
SINCE ALL THINGS ARE PREDETERMINED, I DO NOT GAMBLE.
THEN GAMBLE THAT THEY'RE NOT, AND YOU CAN'T LOSE.
ANOTHER GLASS OF TESTOSTERONE, ANYONE?

CALIFORNIA.
JILL?
I'M LEAVING NOW.
I BEG YOU TO COME WITH ME. THERE IS NOTHING TO STAY FOR HERE.
THE ONLY PLACE FROM WHICH TO WATCH THE END OF THE WORLD IS ANOTHER WORLD.
FENRIS IS THE VERY EMBODIMENT OF RUIN AND DESTRUCTION.
AND HE WALKS YOUR EARTH AGAIN FOR A PURPOSE. YOU UNDERSTAND?
THIS THING THAT'S INSIDE YOU CAN BE DRIVEN OUT. YOU'VE ALREADY PROVED THAT.
AND I HAVE-- FRIENDS WHO MIGHT HELP.
THEN THE GODS BE WITH YOU, JILL PRESTO-- PRESENT COMPANY EXCEPTED, FOR BERGELMIR OF THE JOTUN WILL BE FAR AWAY.
BUT I WILL NOT FORGET YOU SOON.

COLORADO.
IDUN. NJORD. LIFTHRASIR. ARE YOU TELLING ME YOU DON'T SEE THE PATTERN?
IT'S EVERYONE WHO WENT TO THAT FUCKING BANQUET OF HIS.
YEAH, WELL I DIDN'T ASK FOR YOUR OPINION.
YOUR OPINION ISN'T WORTH THE SPIT YOU SPEND ON IT.
I DIDN'T ASK FOR MORE COALS.
NO SIR, BUT IT'S TEN O'CLOCK.
I HAVE TO DO THIS ON THE DOT. I'M SORRY, SIR.
THEN DO IT AND GET THE FUCK OUT.
I WILL, SIR.
NOT A PROBLEM, SIR.
GODDAMN MORON.
SSSSSSSSSS

YES. THE RECONCILIATION DINNER. THE BIG GROUP HUG.
WHAT? WELL MAYBE HE CHANGED HIS MIND.
NO. I LENT MY MIND TO YOU, SKULD. THAT WAS WHAT YOU ATE, WHEN YOU ATE AT MY TABLE.
MY FLESH. MY SOUL. MY MEMORIES.
AND NOW I NEED THEM BACK.

YOU DON'T NEED TO STAND THERE WITH YOUR LIPS PURSED, ABONSAM.

YOU CAN ALWAYS LOOK AWAY. OR GO AND DO SOMETHING USEFUL.

IT'S TRUE I FIND THIS WASTEFUL. BUT I KNOW WHY IT WAS NECESSARY.

LEAVE THE REMAINING GODLINGS TO ME.
IF WE'RE TO GET TO WHERE WE'RE GOING, WE NEED TO PREPARE OUR CHARIOT, TOO.

BRING ME THE MADMAN.

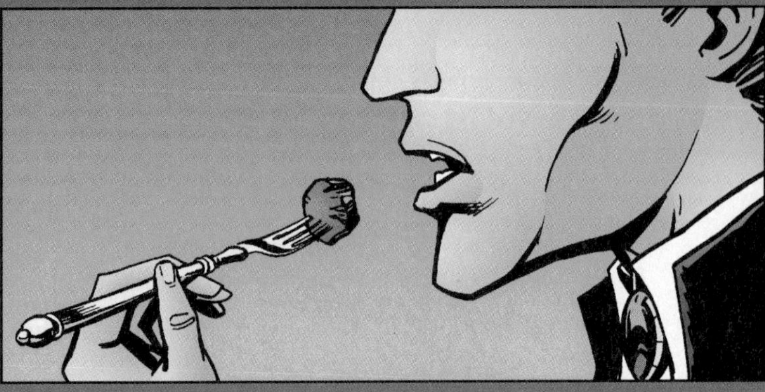

SO-- UMM-- ARE THINGS GETTING BACK TO NORMAL NOW IN THE SILVER CITY?
I MEAN, AFTER THE DAMAGE THE TITANS CAUSED?

THE TERM NORMAL NO LONGER HAS A MEANING, ELAINE.
GOD HAS ABANDONED US, AND AS A RESULT THE WHOLE OF CREATION IS BEGINNING TO UNRAVEL.

IT-- IT IS? I DIDN'T HEAR ABOUT THAT.
IS THAT TRUE?

ONLY YAHWEH'S CREATION. IT DEPENDS ON THE LOGOS-- THE WORD OF GOD-- FOR ITS EXISTENCE.
MY OWN COSMOS WON'T BE AFFECTED.

AND THEREFORE IT DOES NOT MATTER.
AS ANYTHING THAT DOES NOT TOUCH YOU DOES NOT MATTER, LUCIFER.

BUT IF THIS IS THE END OF EVERYTHING, YOU'D KNOW, WOULDN'T YOU?
I MEAN, WE'D BE ON THE LAST PAGE OF THE BOOK.
YES. I WOULD KNOW.

THAT WAS PRECISELY WHY I CAME. TO KNOW WHETHER CREATION CAN BE SAVED.
WHETHER THERE IS ANY POINT IN FURTHER STRIVING.
IT SEEMS LIKE A VERY FAIR QUESTION.
PERHAPS. I HAVE NO OPINION IN THAT REGARD.
BUT FAIR OR UNFAIR, I CHOOSE NOT TO ANSWER IT.

TO READ ALOUD FROM THE BOOK MAKES THE BOOK AN ELEMENT IN THE STORY IT TELLS.
THE DANGER INHERENT IN THAT IS AS GREAT AS THE THREAT YOU SEEK TO ADDRESS.

THAT THIS IS A TURNING POINT IN THE HISTORY OF CREATION IS SELF-EVIDENT.
THE VERY SCRIPT IN WHICH THE BOOK IS WRITTEN CHANGES AFTER THIS POINT.

AT SUCH A JUNCTURE, THE SLIGHTEST WORD OR GESTURE COULD TIP THE BALANCE.

THEN THERE ARE MORE PAGES TO COME.
EVERYTHING TURNS OUT--
THE SCRIPT?
YOU SAY THE SCRIPT IS TO CHANGE? IS THIS NOW? SOON?
MY WORDS WERE THOUGHTLESSLY SPOKEN, ARCHON.
PAY THEM NO HEED.
PLEASE-- EXCUSE ME. I'D LIKE TO TALK TO HIM.
THANKS FOR YOUR HOSPITALITY.
YOU ARE WELCOME, ELAINE BELLOC. IT WAS SCANT ENOUGH.
DAD! WAIT!
and then there were two.
as you intended from the start.

AT LAST THE NIGHT COMES.
TWENTY SECURE.
TWENTY'S WHAT I'M HEARING.
LIGHTS OUT ON FOUR.
AND THEY FADE THE LIGHTS DOWN SO WE CAN SEE WHAT'S UNDERNEATH.
MY NEED FOR HER IS WHAT BRINGS ME HERE.
THE WAY SHE ALWAYS HELD ME, WHEN I WAS SCARED.
THE WAY SHE TOUCHED MY FACE, LIKE I WAS FRAGILE AND SHE WAS SCARED OF BREAKING ME.
AND SHE'S HERE!
SWEET JESUS SHE'S HERE!

SARAH!
SARAH, IT'S ME! IT'S ME!
OH GOD, I WAS REALLY STARTING TO WORRY ABOUT YOU.
IT'S BEEN SO LONG, AND THE DOCTOR SAID YOU WERE DEAD, BUT I KNEW--
WELL THAT WAS A MEAN THING TO SAY.
UNLESS-- YOU KNOW-- IT WAS TRUE, OR SOMETHING.
YOU'RE NOT SARAH.
NOT USUALLY. I MEAN, SOME DAYS IT GETS SO YOU FEEL LIKE YOU'RE PRETTY MUCH EVERYBODY.
IT'S BECAUSE I THINK IN DIFFERENT VOICES. I HAD A FISH ONCE, BUT IT DIDN'T REALLY HELP.
I'M PRETTY ANGRY WITH SOMEBODY.
I HOPE

RATCH
TCHIK

THIS IS REALLY *EXTRAORDINARY.* TRANSFERRING A PRISONER IN THE MIDDLE OF THE *NIGHT.*
DON'T LOOK AT *ME,* MAN. I JUST *WORK* HERE.

I MEAN, WHAT'S THE *RUSH?*
ACCESS TO *COUNSEL.* HIS ATTORNEY ARGUED THAT A SIXTEEN HUNDRED MILE ROUND TRIP DIDN'T *CUT* IT.
WANTS TO TALK TO HIM ABOUT THE *APPEAL* OR SOMETHING.

BUT-- GILMOUR HASN'T *LODGED* AN APPEAL.
THE PAPERWORK WOULD HAVE TO GO THROUGH *ME.*
WELL, THAT'S TOO *BAD.* IT REALLY IS.

IF YOU'D BEEN JUST A *LITTLE* MORE STUPID, DR. SPEARS--
--YOU MIGHT HAVE LIVED TO BE A WHOLE LOT *OLDER.*

I GET ANGRY SOMETIMES, AND I DO *SCARY* THINGS. AT LEAST I *THINK* I DO.

OR MAYBE THAT'S MY *BROTHER.* THIS IS A *NICE* PLACE. NOT TOO COLD, NOT TOO ORANGE. IT REMINDS ME OF AN *OCEAN* I MADE ONCE.

IT WASN'T REAL.
IT WASN'T HER.
I'M STUCK BETWEEN THESE WALLS, IN THIS HOUSE WHERE SHE'S NEVER LIVED.
AND I'M SEEING THINGS THAT *AREN'T* THERE AGAIN.
BECAUSE OTHERWISE MY DOOR IS OPEN. AND I CAN JUST--
HI, CHARLIE.
WE'VE COME TO TAKE YOU TO THE *REAL* WORLD.

IT'S REALLY NOTHING PERSONAL.
I FIND YOU OFFENSIVE AS A CONCEPT.
EVEN THOUGH I KNOW YOU'RE REALLY JUST A SIDE EFFECT.
INDEED? OF WHAT?
OF MY FATHER. OR RATHER, HIS DETERMINISTIC APPROACH TO THE ACT OF CREATION.
CAUSE AND EFFECT ARE USEFUL TOOLS. BUT THEY'RE NOT THE FOUNDATION YOU BUILD ON.
NOT UNLESS YOU WANT TO BUILD A PRISON.
I DO NOT SEE THE ANALOGY. BUT MY OWN PREFERENCE WOULD ALWAYS FAVOR A PRISON--
--OVER, SAY, AN ASYLUM.
AND NOW IT DOES BEGIN TO BE PERSONAL.
YOU'RE TALKING ABOUT MY CREATION.
I AM EXPLORING YOUR METAPHOR. THAT IS ALL.

FORGET THE METAPHOR.
LET ME USE A VISUAL AID.
RRRIP

AND NOW WE'RE BOTH IN THE DARK.
NO.
NOW YOU LOOK AT THE ASHES.
FENRIS YGGDRASIL
AND NOW YOU CHANGE YOUR MIND.

"YOU MUST TELL US EVERYTHING."
"I-- I'LL TRY."
MICHAEL!
MICHAEL, STOP!
"BECAUSE WE NEED TO UNDERSTAND THIS."
"YES. I KNOW."
"I CAUGHT UP WITH HIM ON THE OUTSKIRTS OF HEAVEN."
"I CALLED OUT TO HIM TO STOP."
FATHER!
"AND HE TURNED TO LOOK AT ME."
YOU'VE THOUGHT OF A WAY TO HOLD THE UNIVERSE TOGETHER.
TELL ME WHAT IT IS, AT LEAST. IN CASE IT GOES WRONG. IN CASE SOMETHING HAPPENS TO YOU.
CHILD. ELAINE. GO FROM THIS PLACE.
I BLESS THE PATH THAT LIES BEFORE YOU.
AND I WOULD THAT I HAD KNOWN YOU BETTER.

"I FOLLOWED HIM *INSIDE.* AND I OPENED MY MOUTH TO *SPEAK,* BUT THEN--
"--THERE WAS NO *POINT.* IT WAS TOO *LATE* TO SPEAK.
"THE ROOM WAS FULL OF VOICES. THE *SAME* VOICE, OVER AND OVER ITSELF, A MILLION *TIMES.*
"AND I WAS HEARING IT WITH MY WHOLE *BODY.* I CAN'T DESCRIBE IT. IT WAS-- TERRIBLE.
IT WAS *GOD.* THAT ROOM IS CALLED THE *LOGOS,* AND IT IS WHERE HIS WORDS LIVE.
GO *ON.*
I'M NOT SURE THAT I *CAN* GO ON.
I'M NOT SURE THAT I CAN *EXPLAIN* IT.
"HE LAY DOWN ON THE FLOOR. IN THAT-- PLACE FULL OF NOTHING BUT *NOISE.*
"CURLED *UP* LIKE A CHILD.
"HE CLOSED HIS *EYES,* AND HE--
"--HE *SLEPT.* HE WENT TO SLEEP."

"AND THE POWER THAT WAS IN HIM SPILLED OUT THROUGH THE UNIVERSE.
"AND BECAME US ALL."
THE WOLF BENEATH THE TREE
PART 3 OF 4
MIKE CAREY Writer
PETER GROSS & RYAN KELLY Artists
JARED K. FLETCHER- Lettering
DANIEL VOZZO- Colors and Separations
MICHAEL WM. KALUTA- Cover Painter
MARIAH HUEHNER- Editor
Based on characters created by GAIMAN, KIETH and DRINGENBERG

I DO NOT UNDERSTAND.
I THINK I DO, A LITTLE.
THANK YOU, ELAINE BELLOC, FOR TEACHING ME THIS MYSTERY.
EXAMINE YOUR OWN SUBSTANCE. OR THAT OF ANYTHING YOU SEE--STARS, STONES, WATER, AIR--
LOOK CLOSE ENOUGH AND YOU WILL SEE MICHAEL'S WILL WORKING THERE.
THAT IS IMPOSSIBLE! WHAT YOU SUGGEST, ONLY GOD CAN DO.
HE IS THE DEMIURGE. GOD CHOSE HIM AS HIS SECOND.
NOW, AS GOD'S MARK FADES AND CREATION FALTERS, MICHAEL RENEWS IT MOMENT BY MOMENT.
HE WRITES GOD'S NAME AFRESH ON EVERY ATOM OF EXISTENCE.
INCREDIBLE. BY THIS SACRIFICE, HE--
CALL IT WHAT YOU WILL, URIEL.
THE WOLF IS AT THE DOOR.
AND IT'S NOT GOING TO WORK.

I'M IN A *DREAM.*

FENRIS.

IT TASTES-- NOT LIKE MEAT. LIKE SOMETHING ELSE. LIKE SPICES.
SARAH RUBBED OIL OF CLOVES ONTO MY GUMS ONCE, WHEN I HAD A TOOTHACHE. IT TASTES LIKE THAT.

FOR A MOMENT.

BUT THEN THERE ARE NO MOMENTS.
THE WORLD ROARS, AND I ROAR WITH IT.
I AM DEATH'S GODHEAD! I AM THE WOLF!

I GAVE A BANQUET. DO YOU SEE? I INVITED MY ENEMIES TO EAT WITH ME AND MAKE PEACE.
I FED THEM MY OWN FLESH. IMBUED WITH MY MIND AND MEANING. MY POTENCY.

TO KEEP IT SAFE. UNTIL I CAME TO TAKE IT BACK.
S-- SAFE FROM WHAT?
FROM MYSELF, LITTLE MAD-MAN. FOR I AM DISSOLUTION, AND IN THE TIME OF THE DAWNING, NOTHING WITHSTOOD MY POWER.

AND LO, IN THE TIME OF TWILIGHT--
--SO IT IS AGAIN.

LUCIFER, YOU MUST NOT DO THIS! THE ARCHON IS TRYING TO SAVE US ALL.
TO SHORE UP CREATION BEFORE IT FALLS APART!
I KNOW.
IT MIGHT EVEN WORK, UNDER OTHER CIRCUMSTANCES. BUT I LOOKED OVER DESTINY'S SHOULDER, AND I READ HOW THIS ENDS.
FENRIS IS GOING TO YGGDRASIL. ALL BETS ARE OFF.

MICHAEL, WAKE UP. I NEED TO TALK TO YOU.
MICHAEL!

ALL RIGHT.

THEN WE'LL DO THIS ANOTHER WAY.

WHY SHOULD THIS EVEN CONCERN YOU, MORNINGSTAR?
IT IS HEAVEN'S BUSINESS. LEAVE HEAVEN TO ANSWER IT.
DON'T BE DENSE, URIEL. YGGDRASIL IS ONE OF THE BEGINNING PLACES.

IF CREATION WERE A LENS, THAT WOULD BE ITS FOCAL POINT.
I WAS PREPARED TO SIT OUT THE END OF MY FATHER'S COSMOS--

YOU WERE PREPARED--?

--BUT THE CONFLAGRATION FENRIS INTENDS MIGHT SHAKE MY OWN REALM, TOO.
STAND AWAY FROM THE TOWER.

OR FLY AWAY.
THAT WOULD PROBABLY BE AN EVEN BETTER IDEA.

BAROOM

--YOU WILL NOT SPEAK *AGAIN.*

WHY?
WHY WHAT?

THE *SCARS.*
WHAT ARE THEY *FOR?*

I WILL *DIE* SOON, BET JO'GIE.
I, THE TRICKSTER, WILL DIE. AND IN DEATH WEAVE MY *GREATEST* TRICK.

THIS IS MY *MOCKERY* OF DEATH. OF ENDING.
I DRESS MYSELF IN MY OWN *BLOOD.*

LET'S *FUCK.*

LOOK.
THIS IS *YGGDRASIL,* THE WORLD TREE. YOU'VE SEEN IT BEFORE.

ALTHOUGH IN TRUTH THAT WAS ONLY AN *IMAGE* ABONSAM PLACED IN YOUR MIND.

DO YOU KNOW THE *WAY* THERE, LITTLE MADMAN?
LITTLE MURDERER?
NO.

YOU GET THERE BY *LOSING* YOURSELF.
AND YOU OF ALL PEOPLE KNOW HOW EASY *THAT* CAN BE.

THE JOURNEY IS A SUBTRACTION. A SIMPLIFICATION. LIKE BEING BORN--
--IF YOUR MOTHER'S WOMB WERE WALLED WITH RESTLESS KNIVES.

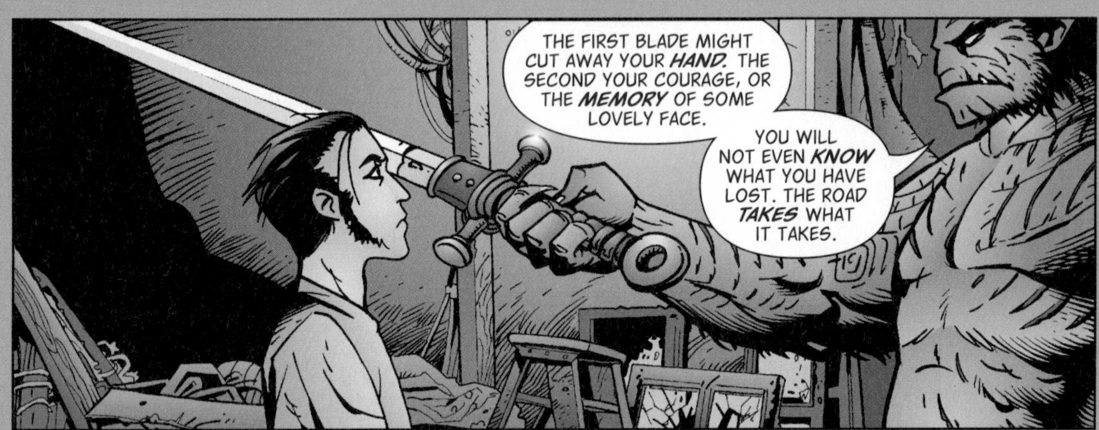
THE FIRST BLADE MIGHT CUT AWAY YOUR HAND. THE SECOND YOUR COURAGE, OR THE MEMORY OF SOME LOVELY FACE.
YOU WILL NOT EVEN KNOW WHAT YOU HAVE LOST. THE ROAD TAKES WHAT IT TAKES.

BUT NOT FROM ME.
FOR YOU WILL BE MY CHARIOT, AND BEAR ME UNHARMED TO YGGDRASIL.

WHY ME? AND WHY WOULD I LET YOU DO THAT?
I CHOSE YOU BECAUSE OF YOUR DISEASE. YOU ARE WELL USED TO SURRENDERING PARTS OF YOURSELF.
THEREFORE YOU WILL BEAR US SWIFTLY. AND FOR THE REST--

YOU WILL SEE YOUR WIFE AND CHILD AGAIN, THERE.
IS THAT NOT WORTH A LITTLE PAIN?

SVARTALFHEIM.
NOW.
URIEL. ESTABLISH A PERIMETER.
DON'T LET ANYTHING DISTURB US.
IF THE JOURNEY ISN'T A PHYSICAL ONE, THEN WHY COME HERE?
BECAUSE THE TREE EXPECTS TO BE APPROACHED FROM THIS DIRECTION.
IT SHOULD MAKE THINGS A LITTLE EASIER.
OF COURSE, THAT'S A RELATIVE TERM.
THERE IS NO EASY WAY OF DOING THIS.

"at least, none that *I've* heard of."

CLOSE YOUR *EYES.*

YOU KNOW WHAT THE TREE *LOOKS* LIKE. YOU HAVE SMELLED THE *AIR* OF THAT PLACE.

TO *WANT* TO GO THERE IS ENOUGH.

IT COMES HARD.
IT
COMES
SLOW.
NOT THE TREE. I LOOK FOR THAT PLACE.
NOTHING.
I GROPE TOWARDS IT.
NOWHERE.
EXCELLENT!
YOU SEE, ABONSAM?
I SEE THE ROAD-- BUT NOT THE END OF IT.
BUT HER FACE IS THE KEY--
--THAT UNLOCKS ME--
AND
TEARS
ME
APART!

MY EARDRUMS BURST AND MEMORIES HEMORRHAGE OUT.
AND. OR.
I WALK FORWARD, AND PARTS OF ME STAY WHERE THEY WERE.
TEAR HOLES IN ME THAT SHOW DAYLIGHT CLEAR THROUGH.
THREE ANGELS FOLLOW ME. THE BRIGHT ONE BLEEDS POWER. THE DARK ONE BLEEDS WILL.
THE SMALLEST MERELY WEEPS. UNLESS THE FLUID THAT LEAKS FROM HER EYES IS SOMETHING ELSE.
AND THEIR STEPS SLOW, UNTIL I SEE THEM NO MORE.

--WHAT I LIKE MOST ABOUT YOU, CHARLIE. YOU NEVER--
TOWER.
OWER!
"YOU MUST REMEMBER THIS--"
YES!
OH YES.
YOU'RE DAMN RIGHT IT'S A BIG DEFICIT.
IN OREGON THEY'RE CLOSING THE SCHOOLS ONE DAY A--
(X+2)(X
WE CAN EXPRESS THIS AS X MINUS TWO.
X-2
PUT UP OR SHUT UP, MAN.
--EXTREME EMOTIONAL DISSOCIATION, WHICH IS A SYMPTOM OF--

YOU'VE DONE WELL, MADMAN.
A FEW STEPS MORE. ONE FINAL EFFORT.
THERE. YOU CAN REST, NOW.
UNTIL YOU'RE NEEDED AGAIN.
NO! NO!
WHERE ARE THEY? WHERE ARE--?
I DON'T REMEMBER THEIR NAMES, BUT WHERE ARE THEY? YOU SAID THEY'D BE HERE!

ALL THAT YOU WANT IS HERE IN THIS BAG I CARRY.
ALL YOU WERE TOLD IS TRUE. REJOICE.
BUT YOU SAID-- THEY'D BE WAITING FOR ME HERE. YOU SAID--
I SAID YOU'D SEE THEM AGAIN, LITTLE MADMAN.
AND SO YOU WILL. SO YOU WILL.

FENRIS. YOU SAW THE ANGELS, CLOSE BEHIND US?
I SAW THEM.
ONE BEHIND AND ONE IN FRONT WOULD BE-- INTERESTING.

THEY'LL COME TOO LATE. TOO WEAK FROM THE JOURNEY.
BECAUSE THEY WALKED WHERE WE RODE. AND IF NOT--

AYE. THEN THERE IS THE TRICK.
AS WE AGREED.

I AM ABONSAM.
MY EYE IS THE HAWK'S EYE. MY HAND STRIKES LIKE A SNAKE.
FROM UNDER YOUR HAND, UNDER YOUR HAMMER I TOOK THEM AWAY.
LEFT DOLLS OF CLAY THAT THOUGHT THEMSELVES ALIVE.
BUT-- WHY DO I LOVE THEM SO MUCH? WHO ARE THEY?
YOUR WIFE. AND YOUR SON.
IN YOUR MADNESS YOU TRIED TO KILL THEM.
BUT ABONSAM SAVED THEM.
I-- THANK YOU! THANK YOU!
NAY, YOU'VE HELPED
TOO.
IN TRUT
THE SCAL
ARE ALMO
EVEN.
I'VE BUT ONE FURTHER FAVOR TO ASK OF YOU.
BUT GATHER YOUR STRENGTH FIRST. THE SWORD IS HEAVY.

YOU'LL HAVE TO TELL ME WHAT TO DO--

YGGRADSIL, THE WORLD TREE. ONE OF THE FOUNDATIONS OF CREATION.

I COULDN'T EVEN SPEAK.

TAKE THE **SWORD--**

--AND **KILL** THEM BOTH.

STRIKE FROM **HERE.**

THE BLOOD OF YOUR WIFE AND SON MUST WATER THE **ROOTS** OF THE TREE.

TO SET THE SEAL UPON THE ENDING OF THE WORLDS.

THE WOLF BENEATH THE TREE PART 4 OF 4

MIKE CAREY Writer

PETER GROSS & RYAN KELLY Artists

JARED K. FLETCHER- Lettering

DANIEL VOZZO- Colors and Separations

MICHAEL WM. KALUTA- Cover Painter

MARIAH HUEHNER- Editor

Based on characters created by GAIMAN, KIETH and DRINGENBERG

NEARBY.
LUCIFER! PLEASE! I KNOW YOU'RE INJURED. REALLY BADLY.
BUT YOU'VE GOT TO WAKE UP!
I CAN'T DO THIS ON MY OWN. I DON'T KNOW IF WE'VE REACHED THE TREE.
I DON'T KNOW WHAT TO DO UNLESS YOU TELL ME.
YOUR FRIENDS ARE HURT. CAN WE DO AUGHT TO HELP?
WHO'S THERE?
WHO ARE YOU?
WE ARE PILGRIMS, ON OUR WAY TO YGGDRASIL. I AM SCEORFAN.
AND THIS MAN HERE IS MY FRIEND, THE HOLY MAN, BERUMIR.
I CAN'T SEE ANYTHING.
I'M BLIND.

THIS IS AN ANGEL. HE LOOKS SCORED AND CORED, SINKING TOWARDS HIS DEATH. BUT YONDER FOUNTAIN--
ITS WATERS HAVE MEDICINAL EFFECTS.
CAN YOU BRING SOME? PLEASE? HE MUSTN'T DIE.
IT'S VERY IMPORTANT THAT WE REACH THE TREE.
AYE, THEN. I'LL FETCH IT IN MY HANDS. WAIT HERE.
PLEASE. BE AS QUICK AS YOU CAN.
DOUBT ME NOT.
SKLLLCHH

HELLO? SCEORFAN? WHAT WAS THAT *SOUND?*
NOTHING.
IT WAS-- NOTHING.

HERE. I *HAVE* THE WATER.
CUP YOUR *HANDS.*

IT-- IT'S *WARM.* IT FEELS LIKE--

QUICKLY. LET IT TRICKLE-- INTO HIS MOUTH--
--ERE HE *DIE* OF HIS WOUNDS.

COF! COF! COF!
LUCIFER! I THINK WE'RE ALMOST *THERE.*
WE'VE JUST GOT TO--
...

DON'T YOU THINK I'M BEAUTIFUL, CHARLIE?
DON'T YOU WANT ME?

KEEP AWAY FROM ME.
OR I SWEAR I'LL KILL YOU.

WITH THIS SWORD YOU MIGHT EVEN MANAGE IT.
BUT BREATHE IN, CHARLIE.

THAT SMELL IS ME. MY HEAT-- MY LOVE FOR YOU.
I AM BET JO'GIE ETTA HI EE. THE WOMAN WHO IS BOTH BEAUTIFUL AND TERRIBLE.
OH GOD. OH GOD.

KILL YOUR WIFE, AND YOUR SON--
AND THEIR BODIES WILL BE THE BED WE COUPLE ON.

I WAS SICK ONCE.
I WAS SICK FOR A LONG TIME. I WAS ON MEDICATION.

AND WHEN I DIDN'T TAKE THE MEDS, I'D GET CONFUSED.
LIKE I DIDN'T ALWAYS KNOW WHAT WAS INSIDE MY HEAD AND WHAT WAS OUTSIDE IT. THAT WAS HOW I FELT RIGHT THEN.

I LOOKED DOWN AT SARAH'S FACE. SO BEAUTIFUL.
BUT I BREATHED IN AGAIN. ANOTHER MOUTHFUL OF HER.
AND I STIRRED AND STIFFENED WITH A TERRIBLE NEED.

UP TO THE HILT, CHARLIE. ALL THE WAY IN, SMOOTH AS SILK.
WON'T THAT FEEL GOOD? WON'T THAT FEEL RIGHT?

OH YES!
GOD, YES!

Hhhhkkkkkk!
L--
LUCIFER?
Hhhhhkkkk!
BROTHER?
ARE YOU
MAD?
LEAVE ELAINE
BE, MORNINGSTAR.
I WARN YOU--
MORNINGSTAR?
I am
FENRIS.
I am
THE
WOLF!

FENRIS--
TELL THE STORY OF THIS, WHEN I AM DEAD.
OF HOW I MADE THIS TRICK.
WHAT? THAT YOU JOINED THE BANQUET OF MY ENEMIES, WHEN I PARCELED MYSELF OUT LIKE BREAD?
THAT YOU TOOK MY ESSENCE INTO YOURSELF-- NOT UNKNOWING, AS THEY DID, BUT WILLINGLY.
SO THAT YOUR BLOOD, NOW PREGNANT WITH MY THOUGHTS, COULD INFECT LORD LUCIFER?
I'LL TELL IT IF I REMEMBER IT.
BROTHER--
--YOU ARE NOT YOURSELF.
SO I AM SORRY FOR THIS.

OH.
PRETTY!
NOT REAL! NOT REAL!
BUT JUST IN CASE--
AAAHHRRR!
SKLUT
SKLUT
SKLUT

IT IS NOT YOU WHO SPEAKS HERE, LUCIFER.
IT IS NOT YOU WHO ACTS.
YOU MUST FIGHT THIS. BECOME YOURSELF AGAIN.
OR OUR WORK AND OUR PAIN IN REACHING THIS PLACE ARE FOR NOTHING-- AND CREATION WILL FALL.
EXCELLENT.

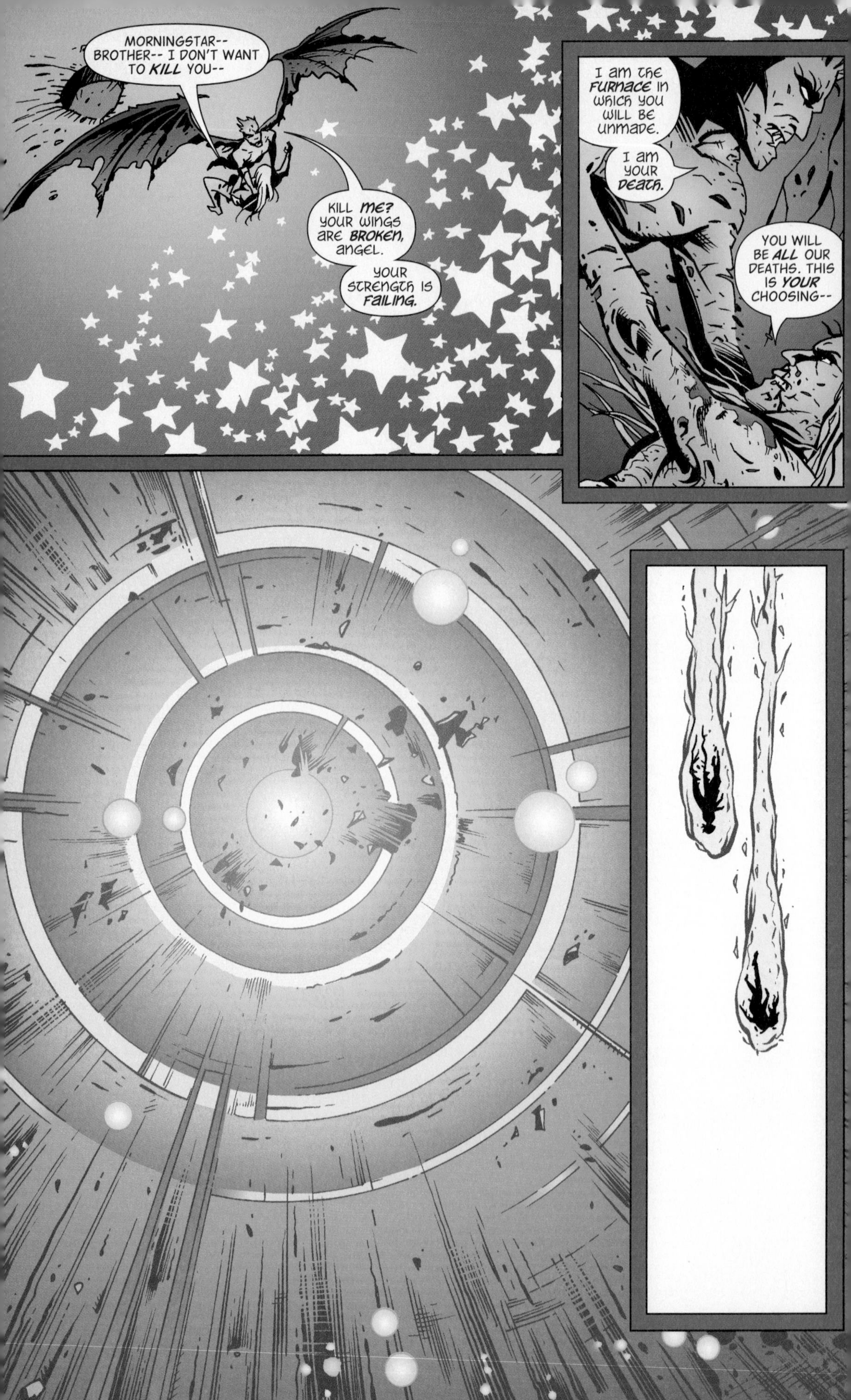
MORNINGSTAR-- BROTHER-- I DON'T WANT TO KILL YOU--
KILL ME? YOUR WINGS ARE BROKEN, ANGEL.
YOUR STRENGTH IS FAILING.
I AM THE FURNACE IN WHICH YOU WILL BE UNMADE.
I AM YOUR DEATH.
YOU WILL BE ALL OUR DEATHS. THIS IS YOUR CHOOSING--

CHARLIE!
SARAH.
CHARLIE, WHAT'S *HAPPENING?*

IT'S ALL RIGHT, SARAH. YOU HAD A BAD *DREAM.*
WE-- WE *ALL* HAD A BAD DREAM. BUT NOW IT'S OKAY.
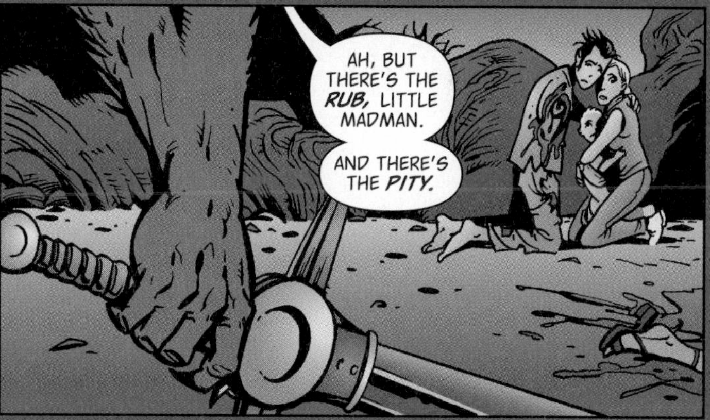
AH, BUT THERE'S THE *RUB,* LITTLE MADMAN.
AND THERE'S THE *PITY.*

THE *DREAM* IS YOUR LIVES.
FROM WHICH YOU WILL AWAKEN INTO A DREAM OF *NOTHING.*

SEE-- THE ROOTS OF THE TREE HAVE BEEN WATERED VERY GENEROUSLY.
BROTHER KILLING BROTHER IS EVERY BIT AS GOOD AS HUSBAND KILLING WIFE, OR FATHER SON.
I WON'T LET YOU HURT THEM.
THEY'RE IRRELEVANT NOW. BUT YOU'RE NOT. YOU WERE THE CHARIOT THAT BROUGHT ME HERE.
NOW YOU'RE THE ANCHOR THAT HOLDS ME.
LO. I CAST OFF--
CHARLIEEE!
--AND I AM GONE.
DO NOT MOURN HIM, WOMAN.
IN THIS TIME OF ENDINGS, HE IS MERELY GONE A LITTLE WAY BEFORE.
THINGS FALL APART.
THE CENTRE CANNOT HOLD.
NOTHING CAN STOP IT NOW.

MICHAEL--
IT IS-- TOO LATE, BROTHER.
WE WERE-- ANTICIPATED-- AND WE HAVE LOST.
I BELIEVE-- I AM DYING.
THAT RAISES PROBLEMS OF ITS OWN, DOESN'T IT?
BRING HER. BRING ELAINE.
I'M HERE, FATHER.

I-- I'LL STAY WITH YOU, IF YOU WANT ME TO. UNTIL--

NO. LISTEN TO ME.
WHILE I CAN STILL SPEAK.

THERE IS A POWER WITHIN ME. THE DUNAMIS DEMIURGOS. GOD'S POWER.
WHEN I DIE, IT WILL POUR OUT OF ME AND OVERWHELM EVERY-THING THAT EXISTS.

BUT--EVERYTHING'S GOING TO FALL APART NOW ANYWAY.
IN DAYS, YES. OR WEEKS.

I'M DYING NOW, ELAINE. YOU HAVE TO TAKE THE POWER FROM ME.

TAKE IT-- TAKE IT FROM YOU?

SHE'S NOT STRONG ENOUGH. IT WILL DESTROY HER.

I CAN THINK OF NO OTHER WAY. EXCHANGE FORGIVENESS WITH ME, LUCIFER.
I AM SORRY THAT IT CAME TO THIS.

YOU DON'T NEED MY FORGIVENESS.

IT WAS MY MISTAKE THAT BROUGHT US HERE.

YOU WILL HAVE TO BE BOTH CONDUIT AND DAM, ELAINE.
TO RECEIVE THE FLOOD, AND THEN TO PEN IT IN, SO THAT IT FINDS ITS LEVEL WITHIN YOU.
I DON'T KNOW HOW. I DON'T KNOW HOW TO DO THAT.
YOU GOTTA GET US OUT OF HERE, MISTER.
MY SON CAN'T TAKE MUCH MORE OF THIS.
AHUH AHUH AHUH
THE WAYS OUT OF HERE ARE ALMOST AS HARD AS THE WAYS IN.
JUST WAIT A WHILE LONGER. IT MAY ALL BECOME ACADEMIC IN A MOMENT OR TWO.
IF YOU SURVIVE THIS, YOU WILL HAVE MANY RESPONSIBILITIES.
BUT I THINK YOU WILL RISE TO THEM. I THINK THERE ARE FEW THINGS THAT YOU CANNOT DO.
FATHER. OH GOD, I'M SORRY I NEVER CAME TO YOU. NEVER TRIED TO TALK--
IT WOULD HAVE DONE NO GOOD. I WAS PROUD, AND STUBBORN.
I COULD HAVE SOUGHT YOU OUT. I COULD HAVE--
AAAHHRRR!

AND THE WORLD WENT AWAY. AND SARAH. AND BOBBY.

I REACHED OUT TO THEM-- TO TELL THEM I WAS OKAY-- BUT MY HAND TOUCHED RED-BROWN EARTH.

NO, NOT EARTH. DUST. DUST SO DRY YOU'D SWEAR IT HAD ***NEVER*** DRUNK.

AND I WANTED TO SAY, NO. I'M NOT DONE YET. I'VE GOT TO MAKE SURE THEY'RE ***SAFE.***

NO.

WELCOME TO YOUR DEATH--
--AND OUR ARMY.
The End

SO THERE'S A WHEEL, ABOUT FOUR HUNDRED, FIVE HUNDRED FEET ACROSS THE MIDDLE.
AND-- STOP ME IF I'M GETTING TOO TECHNICAL-- THE WHEEL TURNS A SCREW.

THIS IS IN GEHENNA. HELL CENTRAL.
YOU SLACK OFF, THEY'VE GOT AN INCENTIVE SCHEME. GUARANTEED TO RE-MOTIVATE YOU.

THE GROUND IS BROKEN GLASS-- SHARP AS A FUCKING RAZOR.
AND SINCE YOU'RE CHAINED TO YOUR POST, FALLING DOWN ON THE JOB IS GONNA GET YOU JULIENNED. NOT RECOMMENDED.

THE SCREW IS A MILL-- LIKE A PEPPER MILL.
SO YOU'RE SCREWING A WHOLE BUNCH OF OTHER GUYS WHO'RE STUCK IN THERE. ECONOMY OF EFFORT, SEE?

AND ONCE EVERY THOUSAND YEARS--
--EVERYONE GETS TO CHANGE PLACES.

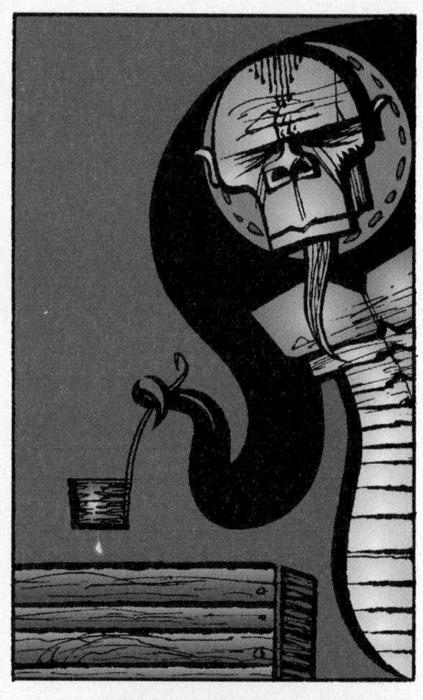

HERE.
DRINK.

YOU'VE GOTTA SEE THIS IN CONTEXT, RIGHT?
BRING HIM!
BRING HIM TO ME!
THESE GUYS SET A LOT OF STORE BY ROUTINE.
AND IN THEIR CASE, IT'S NOT A ROUTINE UNLESS YOU'VE BEEN DOING IT FOR A HUNDRED MILLENNIA OR SO.
WHEN SOMEONE STEPS OUT OF LINE--
--YOU JUST KNOW THERE'S GONNA BE TROUBLE.
THE EIGHTH SIN
MIKE CAREY- WRITER MARC HEMPEL- GUEST ARTIST
JARED K. FLETCHER- LETTERING DANIEL VOZZO- COLORING
MICHAEL WM. KALUTA- COVER PAINTER MARIAH HUEHNER- EDITOR
BASED ON CHARACTERS CREATED BY GAIMAN, KIETH AND DRINGENBERG

WHY DID NOBODY TELL ME ABOUT THIS *BEFORE?*
AND WHY HAVE YOU *ALLOWED* IT TO HAPPEN?
IT WAS AN ISOLATED *INCIDENT,* REMIEL. OF NO SIGNIFICANCE, BEYOND--
FIVE ISOLATED INCIDENTS. IN FIVE DIFFERENT *REGIONS* OF HELL.
WHICH I RULE-- I NEED HARDLY REMIND YOU-- IN *HEAVEN'S* NAME.

WELL, I WAS GONNA HAVE TO LOOK UP SOME OF THE BIG WORDS--

--BUT I GUESS I GOT THE GIST.

YOU KNOW IF I DIDN' EXIST--

--SOMEONE WOULD HAVE T INVENT ME.

DO ME THE COURTESY OF NOT PRETENDING IGNORANCE.
WE ARE THREATENED WITH CRISIS, AND YOUR RESPONSE IS TO WEED THE HERBACEOUS BORDERS.

WELL, IT DOESN'T ABSOLVE YOU DUMA.

IT DOESN'T MEAN YOU CAN WASH YOUR HANDS.

YOU NEVER DO ANYTHING. SO I HAVE TO DO IT ALL!
I HAVE TO MAKE THE HARD CHOICES. I HAVE TO BE CRUEL, SO THAT YOU CAN STAY CLEAN!

YAHWEH HAS ABANDONED US!
WHAT ARE WE, THEN? WHAT ARE WE WITHOUT HIM?

A MARIGOLD. THAT SYMBOLIZES MOURNING, DOES IT NOT?
WELL CERTES, WE HAVE MUCH TO MOURN.

I'M SORRY I DISTURBED YOU, BROTHER.
I KNOW HOW PRECIOUS YOUR TIME IS.

BEHOLD, I BREAK THIS BREAD AND PASS IT AMONG YOU.
TASTE IT, AND CONSIDER.

WHEN WE EAT, WE TAKE INTO OURSELVES THAT WHICH IS NOT US.
THEN BY THE ACTION OF OUR STOMACH AND OUR BOWELS WE ASSIMILATE IT, SO THAT IT BECOMES A PART OF US.

IN THE SAME WAY, THIS HELL WHERE WE LIVE IS A STOMACH--
--THAT DIGESTS US AND MAKES US OVER INTO ITS OWN IMAGE.

THIS IS A SINGLE INSTANCE OF A UNIVERSAL LAW. FROM MOMENT TO MOMENT, WE CHANGE. WE BECOME.
IF WE ARE ANYTHING AT ALL, WE ARE THAT BECOMING.

LIKE LUCIFER, WHO FELL FROM HEAVEN TO HELL, AND THEN ROSE AGAIN.
TO SHOW US THE WAY. TO SHOW US HOW SHORT ETERNITY IS.

WHAT WOULD YOU KNOW OF LUCIFER? YOU NEVER FOUGHT WITH HIM. FELL WITH HIM.
HE WAS NEVER YOUR COMMANDER, OR YOUR BROTHER, CHRISTOPHER RUDD.

WHEN HE DUELED WITH AMENADIEL OF THE THRONES, I WAS ALL THE ARMY HE HAD.
I CARRIED HIS HEART IN MY HANDS.

YOU-- YOU WERE WITH HIM THEN?
I SAVED HIM THEN. I DELIVERED HIS ENEMY INTO HIS POWER.
THE MORNINGSTAR IS MY PATRON, AND MY FRIEND.

THEN I LAY DOWN MY ARMS AT YOUR FETT. AND MY LIFE, TOO, IF YOU WISH IT.
I AM YOURS. WHAT WOULD YOU HAVE ME DO?

EAT.
AND BELIEVE.
AND BE RENEWED.

TEACHER, THERE IS A WOMAN WHO WOULD SPEAK WITH YOU.
LET HER COME, TROHAIN.
BUT FOR A MOMENT, ONLY. I'LL SPEAK AGAIN WHILE MY WORDS ARE STILL IN THEIR MINDS.

SHE SAYS YOUR CONVERSE MUST BE PRIVATE, TEACHER.
LIKE THE COMMUNION YOU GAVE HER IN LORD ARUX'S HOUSE, THE NIGHT IT BURNED.

TELL THE OTHERS TO WAIT.
IF THEY GROW RESTLESS, LEAD THEM IN A SONG.

LYS.
MILORD RUDD.
HOW DOES YOUR HONOR FOR THIS MANY A DAY?

IF YOU MEANT THE QUESTION SERIOUSLY, I'M WELL. THANK YOU.
AND YOURSELF?
I WAX. I FLOURISH. WHEN YOU BETRAYED MY FATHER, YOU DID ME A GREAT SERVICE.

I HAVE DONE YOU NOTHING BUT HARM. BECAUSE BOTH MY LOVE AND MY HATE FOR YOU WERE SELFISH.
AND MY PUNISHMENT IS TO LOVE YOU STILL. WITHOUT HOPE.

AH, BUT TO RUT WITH A DEMON-- WOULD THAT NOT STEEP YOUR SOUL IN MORTAL SIN AGAIN?
THERE IS NO MORTAL SIN.
THERE ARE ONLY SOULS, LOST IN A MAZE THAT SOMEONE ELSE HAS MADE FOR THEM.

THEN LET'S WALK DOWN BY THE RIVER, CHRISTOPHER, WHERE WE WON'T BE SEEN--
AND YOU CAN UNDO ME BEFORE YOU UNDO HELL.
LYS--
FLUTTER FLUTTER FLUTTER.
RUSTLE RUSTLE.
LOUD THROAT-CLEARING NOISE.

GAUDIUM.
OH GOOD, YOU CAN SEE ME.
I WAS SCARED SHE MIGHT'VE PUT YOUR EYES OUT WITH THOSE THINGS.
THE BIG GUY OWES YOU A FAVOR, AND I GUESS I'M IT. READ IT AND WEEP, PAL.
HER LADYSHIP JUST TOOK A BRIEFING FROM SOME GUYS WITH FEATHERS.
I'M SURROUNDED BY MY FOLLOWERS HERE, LADY.
DID YOU TRULY THINK YOU COULD TAKE ME OUT FROM AMONG THEM?
AH, IT IS MY PRIDE, CHRISTOPHER. I LOVE YOU TOO, YOU SEE.
BUT MY PRIDE WILL NEVER ALLOW ME TO TAKE YOU--
--EXCEPT FROM ON TOP.

AND THE CHERUB, LADYSHIP?
THE CHERUB'S GONNA FOLD YOU INTO A PAPER KITE, YOU PIECE OF--GNNNNRRRRR! YOU'RE GONNA WEEP BLOOD FOR THIS! YOU'RE GONNA--
STUFF HIM AND MOUNT HIM. THERE'S PROBABLY A SPACE IN THE PARLOR.

"PAIN IS A *LADDER,* CHRISTOPHER RUDD, BY WHICH A PILGRIM SOUL MAY ASCEND TO *HEAVEN."*
"WHEN YOU *INTERRUPT* THAT PROCESS, YOU SET YOURSELF AGAINST THE WILL OF *GOD."*

GOD IS *DEAD.*
A *COMMON* MISCONCEPTION. HE IS GONE, BUT HE WILL *RETURN.*
IN THE MEANTIME, WE EMBODY HIS *PLAN* AND HIS *AUTHORITY.*

THROUGH US, HIS GREAT *WORK* GOES ON.
THROUGH US, HIS *LOVE* ENFOLDS EVEN THOSE WHO TRY HARDEST TO REJECT IT.

NO. THE *TORTURE* YOU INFLICT HAS BECOME AN END IN ITSELF, REMIEL.
AND YOUR EXCESSES WILL BECOME *WORSE* AS YOUR FEAR GROWS. BECAUSE YOU'RE *ALONE* NOW, AND YOU'RE AFRAID THAT--

SMACK
YOU ARE *MISTAKEN.*
YOU SPEAK ABOUT THINGS *FAR* BEYOND YOUR UNDER-STANDING.

HE IS ONE OF THE *DAMNED,* IS HE NOT?
AYE, MY LORD.
FROM WHAT *PROVINCE?*

FROM *EFFRUL,* MY LORD. AND THE LADY LYS HAS OFFERED TO TAKE HIM *BACK.*
TO TAKE THE *RESPONSIBILITY* FOR HIS PUNISHMENT HERSELF.

HE-- IS-- *NOT--* BEING-- *PUNISHED.*

HE HAS *SINNED.* GRIEVOUSLY. BUT THROUGH HIS *SUFFERING* HIS GUILT MAY BE BURNED AWAY.
AND HIS SOUL BE WASHED *CLEAN* IN BLOOD. YOU *SEE* THIS?
YES, MY LORD.

THEN TAKE HIM *AWAY,* TO THE PLACES WHERE YOU PEOPLE *WORK.*
AND *REDEEM* HIM.

IF THIS WERE A MOVIE, I THINK BY NOW WE'D HAVE REACHED THE END OF THE SECOND ACT.
HOW DO I WHAT?
I SAID, HOW DO YOU STUFF A CHERUB?
TAP TAP

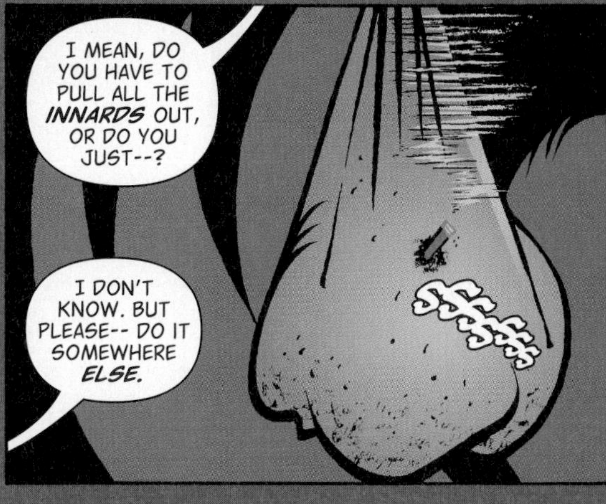
I MEAN, DO YOU HAVE TO PULL ALL THE INNARDS OUT, OR DO YOU JUST--?
I DON'T KNOW. BUT PLEASE-- DO IT SOMEWHERE ELSE.
SSSSSS

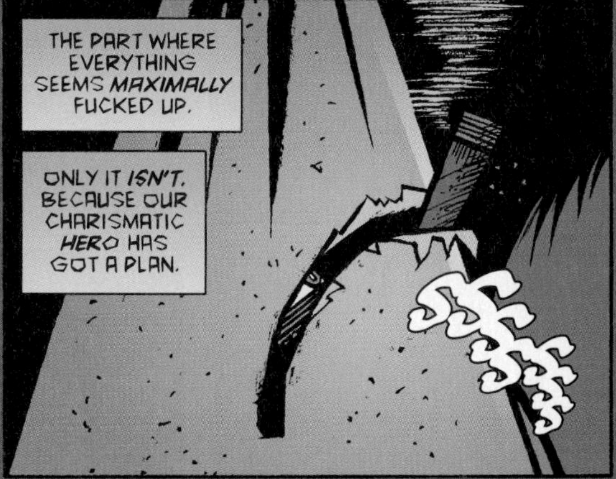
THE PART WHERE EVERYTHING SEEMS MAXIMALLY FUCKED UP.
ONLY IT ISN'T. BECAUSE OUR CHARISMATIC HERO HAS GOT A PLAN.
SSSSSS

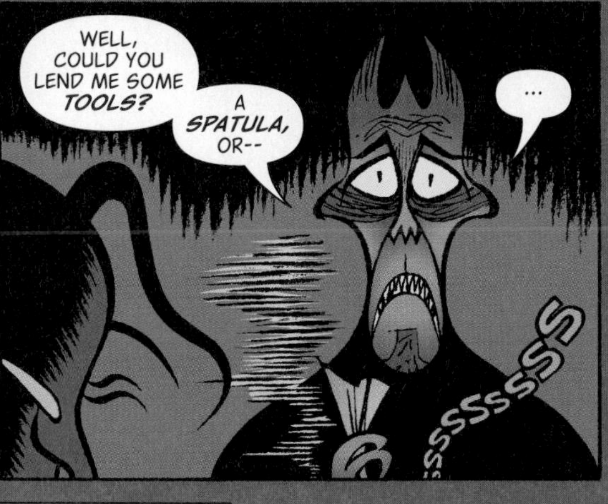
WELL, COULD YOU LEND ME SOME TOOLS?
A SPATULA, OR--
...
SSSSSSSSS

AAAURGH!

BUT BECAUSE I'M MORE CHARISMATIC THAN MOST, I FIGURE IT'S OKAY IF I JUST MAKE IT UP AS I GO ALONG.
TO SWITCH METAPHORS, IT WAS THE BOTTOM OF THE NINTH AND THE BASES WERE TOWERING INFERNOS. WHO'S GONNA STEP UP TO THE PLATE?
WHO ELSE?

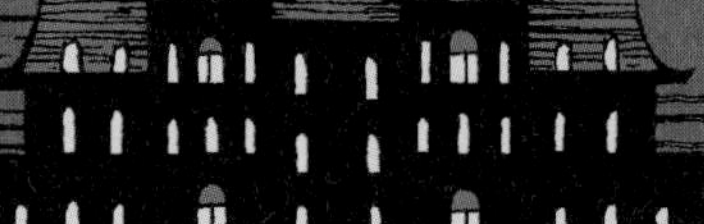

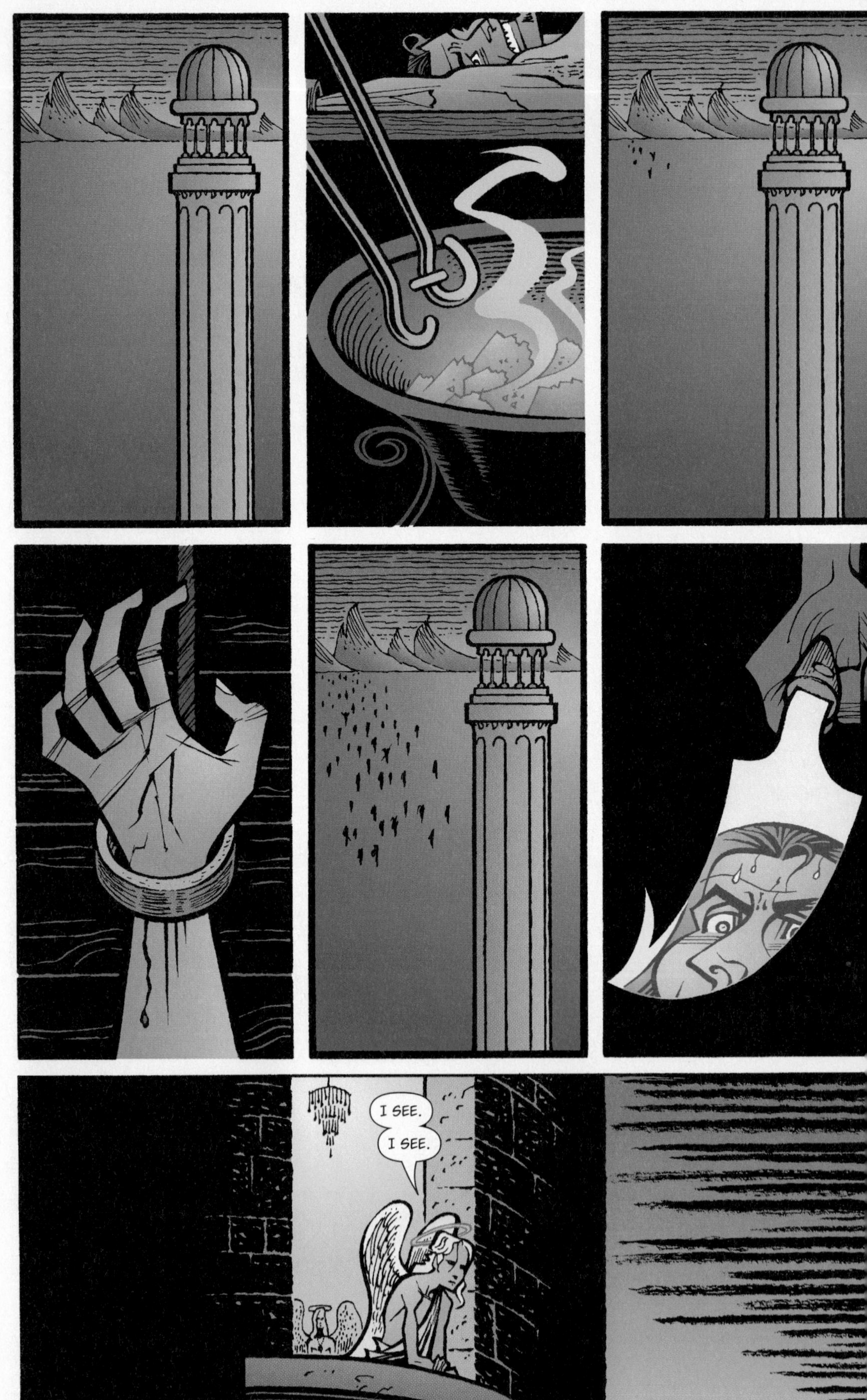
I SEE.
I SEE.

THE SOUL IS ETERNAL, CHRISTOPHER RUDD. BUT ITS STRANDS MAY BE UNPICKED AND SEPARATED.
THAT IS THE DEATH THAT WAITS BEHIND DEATH. THE DEATH WITH NO FURTHER SHORE.

TELL YOUR FOLLOWERS THAT YOU WERE WRONG. EXPLAIN TO THEM THE NECESSITY FOR HELL'S EXISTENCE.
OR THIS ENDLESS DYING WILL BE YOUR FATE.

I WAS WRONG IN ONE RESPECT ONLY. I TOLD THE LADY LYS THAT THERE WAS NO SIN.
BUT THERE IS.

HELL ITSELF IS A SIN.
YOU WILL NOT BE FORGIVEN FOR IT.

VERY WELL.
YOUR LAST SERMON SHALL BE WITHOUT WORDS.

THE RULE OF HEAVEN IS THE RULE OF *LAW,* AND *REASON.*
YOU *WILL* LISTEN TO REASON.

HERE. NOW. BY *RIGHT* AND ORDINANCE DIVINE, I PASS *SENTENCE* ON YOUR TEACHER.
HIS SOUL I WILL *DIVIDE* INTO AS MANY PIECES AS HE HAS DISCIPLES. AND I WILL *CAST* THE PIECES FROM THE ROOF OF THIS TOWER.

THAT YOU MAY HEAR A NEW *GOSPEL* IN THE SHRIEKING OF THE WIND--
--AND A *SERMON* IN THE THUNDER.

AAAHHRRRR!

DUMA? WHAT--?
YOU ARE RIGHT, MY BROTHER.
THIS THING IS TOO HARD. THIS CUP MUST PASS FROM YOU.

BUT-- YOU HAVE SPOKEN! BEFORE THESE FALLEN CREATURES YOU HAVE BROKEN FAITH WITH YOUR CREATOR.
IT IS NOT BROKEN.
ONLY MOVED, FROM ONE QUARTER INTO ANOTHER.

I AM THE ELDER HERE, REMIEL. I AM THE BEARER OF THE KEY.
THE WEIGHT OF THIS VERDICT FALLS ON ME ALONE.

RULE US, CHRISTOPHER RUDD.
YOU HAVE SHOWN YOURSELF FIT.

SO THEN RUDD PROMISED THERE WAS GONNA BE SOME KIND OF NEW DEAL.
"YOU'VE SEEN THE END OF HELL, AND NOW YOU'RE GONNA SEE THE END OF HEAVEN." STUFF LIKE THAT.
AT LEAST I THINK THAT'S WHAT HE SAID. ON THE OTHER HAND, IT COULD'VE BEEN "THANKS FOR COMING." IT WAS HARD TO HEAR OVER THE SINGING AND THE SHOUTING AND THE SPEAKING IN TONGUES.
AND REMIEL CRYING HIS EYES OUT, LIKE ONE OF THOSE OLD LADIES IN THE BACK ROW AT A WEDDING.
SO WHAT THE HELL, AS THEY SAY DOWN HERE. I MISSED THE CORONATION, BUT I MADE IT TO THE PARTY AFTERWARDS.
SOONER DO IT THAT WAY, TO BE HONEST.
I FUCKING HATE FORMAL OCCASIONS.

ONE TENDS TO SLIP AND *SLIDE* IN THE SOFT PLACES. BUT THE BARROWJANE NAVIGATES THEM VERY *WELL.*

WHEN SHE *BREACHES,* YOU'LL REMEMBER THINGS THAT HAVE YET TO *HAPPEN.* IT CAN BE UNSETTLING, AT FIRST.

"THERE WAS A SENSATION OF *MOVEMENT,* IN NO DIRECTION I COULD *DEFINE.*

"A SINGLE *RIPPLE* STIRRED THE SURFACE OF THE HOT, BROWN *LIQUID* IN MY CUP.

"AND IT *BEGAN.*

"I WAS IN A DIFFERENT *PLACE.*

"THE *MORNINGSTAR,* SAMAEL, WAS EXPLAINING TO THE HOST THAT THE *UNIVERSE* WAS CLOSE TO ITS ENDING.

YAHWEH'S NAME IS WRITTEN ON EVERY *ATOM* OF HIS CREATION. IT'S THE *GLUE* THAT HOLDS REALITY TOGETHER.

NOW THE GLUE ISN'T *HOLDING* AS WELL AS IT DID. WHEN IT'S GONE, YOU WILL BE TOO. ALONG WITH EVERYTHING *ELSE* THAT LIVES HERE.

"IT WAS THE SCHEME OF FENRIS, THE WOLF-- TO WATER THE WORLD-TREE WITH KIN-SHED BLOOD.
"TO MAKE THE DEATH OF ALL THE WORLDS, WHICH WAS ALREADY UNDER WAY, TRULY INEVITABLE.
"HE LEFT THAT PLACE WELL PLEASED WITH ALL HIS WORK.
"BUT THE MORNINGSTAR REMAINED, AS MICHAEL'S DEMIURGIC POWER BLED OUT INTO THE WORLD.
"HE WALKED INTO THE HEART OF THAT TEMPEST.
"NEXT I SAW A WOMAN SCREAMING IN PAIN. THE PAIN OF BIRTH, WHICH I KNOW ONLY TOO WELL.
"BUT HER I DID NOT KNOW, NOR THE THING THAT SCREAMED INSIDE HER.
"AND IN HELL, THE MASSING OF A MIGHTY ARMY. DEMONS AND DAMNED TOGETHER, UNDER THE SAME BANNER.
"A FORCE THE LIKE OF WHICH CREATION HAD NEVER SEEN.
"THE GREAT JUDGE, SOLOMON, TURNED FROM HIS PURPOSE.
"SUMMONED FORTH TO DELIVER ONE FINAL VERDICT IN THE HALLS OF HEAVEN."

BUT HEAVEN'S WALLS WERE *BLEEDING.*
"AND THE HOST OF ALL THE ANGELS COULD NOT *HEAL* THEM."
CRUX
PART 1 OF 2
MIKE CAREY- WRITER
PETER GROSS & RYAN KELLY- ARTISTS
JARED K. FLETCHER- LETTERING
DANIEL VOZZO- COLORS AND SEPARATIONS
MICHAEL WM. KALUTA- COVER PAINTER
MARIAH HUEHNER-EDITOR
BASED ON CHARACTERS CREATED BY
GAIMAN, KIETH AND DRINGENBERG

BUT HOW DID OU COME TO *SEE* L THESE THINGS, MOTHER?

AND WHY RE YOU *TELLING* ME ABOUT THEM NOW?

I DON'T KNOW. BECAUSE LUCIFER'S FATE *CONCERNS* YOU, I SUPPOSE.

AND ALL THESE THINGS COME *BACK* TO HIM, IN THE END.

YOU DIDN'T TELL ME *HIS* FATE.

I TOLD YOU WHAT I *COULD,* MAZIKEEN. NOT ALL THINGS WERE *REVEALED* TO ME.

IF YOU'RE *THIRSTY,* DRINK FROM THIS WELL. THE WATER HERE IS VERY *PURE,* AND VERY COLD.

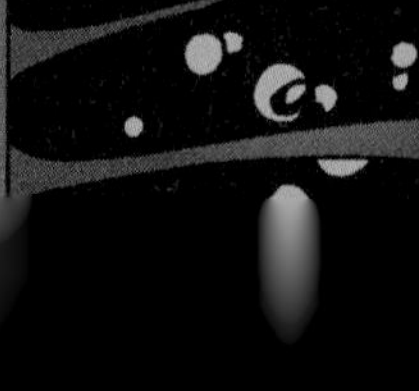

YOU HAVEN'T EMBRACED ME. OR WEPT ON MY SHOULDER.
OR SHOWN ANY OTHER SIGN OF BEING HAPPY TO SEE ME AGAIN.
IT'S BEEN LONG. AND YOU LEFT US OF YOUR OWN FREE WILL.
AND YOU NEVER CAME BACK.
AM I NOT PRECIOUS TO YOU, MAZIKEEN?
AM I NOT REMEMBERED?
YES. YOU ARE REMEMBERED.
WE REMEMBER WHAT YOU TOLD US TO REMEMBER.
THAT HEAVEN HAS WRONGED US. THAT WE EXIST TO AVENGE THAT WRONG. YOU SHAPED US WELL, MOTHER.
SSSUKK

I GAVE YOU LIFE. IS IT WRONG TO ASK FOR LOYALTY?
PERHAPS. I'M PROBABLY NOT THE BEST ONE TO ASK.
THESE DAYS MY LOYALTY IS ENGAGED ELSEWHERE.
WITH THE MORNINGSTAR. YES, I KNOW.
I DON'T BEGRUDGE YOU THAT. BUT I DO QUESTION THE WISDOM OF IT.
THE LILIM ARE NOT FRIENDS OF HEAVEN, OR OF HELL. THEY MAINTAIN THEIR INDEPENDENCE.
EXCEPT FROM YOU, OF COURSE.
COME. HELP ME WITH MY WORK, AND I'LL EXPLAIN TO YOU.
YOU CAN STOP NOW, SYLVIANA.
ATTEND TO YOUR FINAL DUTIES, AS I TAUGHT YOU.
YOU SHOULD KNOW, MAZIKEEN, THAT MATTERS ARE COMING TO A CRUX.
A POINT OF BALANCE.

"IN THE WORLD F MEN, A GREAT NMAKING HAS BEGUN.
"SUBTLY-- AS ALL GREAT THINGS GROW FROM SEEDS TOO SMALL TO NOTICE.
"NOTHING BREAKS, AS YET. NOTHING FALLS.
"BUT THE HANDS OF ARTISTS LOSE THEIR CUNNING. THE MINDS OF MUSICIANS THEIR SWEET CALCULUS.
"AND EMOTION DIES TOO. LOVER LOOKS AT LOVER, PARENT AT CHILD.
"FEELING NOTHING SAVE THE DEAD GREY VOID OF ANOMIE.
"THE WORLD LOSES ITS SAVOR. THE SENSES DULL.
"SWEET, SOUR, BITTER, SALT, ALL BLEED INTO ONE NOTHINGNESS.
"IN SHEER DESPAIR OF FEELING ANYTHING AT ALL, PEOPLE BEGIN TO HURT THEMSELVES."
IT IS AHWEH'S NAME, WRITTEN IN ALL OF US.
WITH AHWEH GONE, IT FADES. AND WE FADE TOO, BY INEXORABLE LOGIC.

YOU'RE VERY WELL INFORMED FOR AN EXILE, MOTHER.
I WOULDN'T HAVE THOUGHT THAT MUCH NEWS REACHED YOU BEHIND YOUR WATERFALL OF SWORDS.
NO. IT DOESN'T.
WHAT I KNOW ABOUT THESE THINGS, I'VE KNOWN FOR A LONG TIME.
JUST AS I'VE KNOWN THAT YOU WOULD COME HERE.
FROM BRIADACH? DID HE PROPHESY FOR YOU, BEFORE YOU LEFT?
HE DIDN'T HAVE THAT GIFT WHEN I LEFT.
THAT CAME LATER.
NO, I SAW THESE THINGS FOR MYSELF.
YOUR COMING INTO LUCIFER'S SERVICE. YOUR JOURNEY HERE.
YOUR DEATH.
MY DEATH?
WELL, IT SEEMED TO ME THAT YOU DIED. YOU WERE IN A DEEP PIT, AND EARTH WAS POURED IN OVER YOU. YOU SCREAMED.
WHEN DID YOU SEE THIS?
THAT'S-- HARDER TO EXPLAIN, MY LOVE.
BUT I'LL TRY.

"AFTER IBRIEL DIED, I FOUND MY USUAL SOLACES DENIED TO ME.
"I HAD LOVED HIM, AND MY OWN CHILDREN HAD KILLED HIM.
"IT WAS HARD FOR ME TO BEAR.
"THAT WAS AN ENDLESS TIME FOR ME. I WATCHED YOU ALL GROW INTO YOUR POWER, AND I OUGHT TO HAVE REJOICED.
"BUT MY HEART WAS BECOME AN EMPTY ROOM, SILTED WITH DUST.
"FINALLY I LEFT. TAKING NOTHING WITH ME. NOT CARING WHETHER I LIVED OR DIED.
"DEATH WAS PREFERABLE TO THIS TEDIOUS LABYRINTH OF GRIEF.
"BUT I REALIZED AS I WALKED THAT HEAVEN HAD CONSPIRED IN MY SUFFERING.
"AND I FOUND THAT MY HATRED OF CRUEL YAHWEH, MY MAKER, MADE THE HURT LESSEN.
"SO I NURTURED IT, AND FED IT. AS I STILL DO.
"I WENT INTO THE SOFT PLACES, WHERE TIME AND SPACE FLOW LIKE WATER.
"I SLEPT UNDER CHANGING SKIES, AND MY SLEEP WAS TROUBLED."

"I WAS AWARE THAT SOMEONE FOLLOWED ME. WATCHED ME.
"HE LEFT FOOD FOR ME SOMETIMES AT THE EDGE OF MY CAMP. AND ONCE HE KILLED A PREDATOR THAT MUST HAVE BEEN HUNTING ME.

"ONE NIGHT I BENT MYSELF TO THE TASK OF FINDING WHERE HE SLEPT.

"AND STOLE UPON HIM UNAWARES AS HE PREPARED YET ANOTHER OFFERING FOR ME."

MOTHER.

BRIADACH.
I-- I WAS WORRIED ABOUT YOU IN THESE WILD PLACES, ALONE.

I CHOSE TO BE ALONE. BUT IF I LOOKED FOR SOCIETY, YOURS WOULD BE THE LAST I'D SEEK.

PATRICIDE.

WE KILLED IBRIEL BECAUSE WE LOVED YOU.
TO AVENGE HIS SLIGHTING OF YOU.
I KNEW THAT. BUT I DIDN'T CARE.
FAMILY HAD ALWAYS BEEN THE THING THAT MATTERED MOST TO ME. YOU. THE ARMY OF MY CHILDREN.
BUT GRIEF HARDENED ME. I SAW THINGS DIFFERENTLY NOW.
"THE SOFT PLACES ARE DOORWAYS INTO CHAOS. INTO THE TIMELESS VOID BEYOND CREATION.
"I WALKED ON INTO CHAOS, AND THE EARTH BEAT LIKE A HEART BENEATH MY FEET.
THE GOING BECAME MORE TREACHEROUS THE FURTHER I WENT. SOLID GROUND COULD NO LONGER BE RELIED ON.
"THE LAWS THAT GOVERN BRUTE MATTER WERE COMING UNDONE.
"I THOUGHT I MUST DIE NOW, AND I WAS NOT AVERSE.
"BUT AS SO OFTEN WHEN MY BACK IS TO THE WALL--"

"--LIFE STRETCHED OUT A *HAND* TO ME."
BJ's
macrobiotic
RESTAURANT

"THE HOUSE WAS *IMPOSSIBLE*. STANDING FIRM AND UNTROUBLED AS *REALITY* BUCKED AND HEAVED AROUND IT.
"THE STRANGE *SIGILS* ON ITS WALLS SEEMING TO PROMISE *EPIPHANIES* AND REVELATIONS.
"I DECIDED TO *GO* THERE.
"AND SEE WHAT *MEANINGS* IT HELD FOR *ME*."
OPEN
LEAVE YOUR HANG-UPS OUT ON THE STREET.

GOOD DAY TO YOU, LILITH OF EDEN GARDEN.
YOU ARE MOST WELCOME HERE.
YOU KNOW ME?
"HE INCLINED HIS HEAD, ON WHICH NO EXPRESSION COULD BE SEEN."
WE ARE HERE EXPRESSLY ON YOUR ACCOUNT.
PLEASE. STEP INSIDE. THE WEATHER IS INCLEMENT.
HAVE YOU A RETINUE?
SERVANTS? COMPANIONS?
NO.
I'M ALONE.
YOU CAN CLOSE THE DOOR.
CLOSED
LEAVE YOUR HANG-UPS OUT ON THE STREET.

"THERE IS NOT MUCH ROOM FOR REGRET IN THE LIFE I'VE CHOSEN.
MOTHER!
"BUT FOR THIS I AM SORRY.
"THAT ALL THOSE MILLENNIA OF PAIN WERE WAITING FOR HIM--
"AND I COULD HAVE SAVED HIM WITH A SINGLE WORD.
"YET I DID NOT SPEAK."

HAVE YOU WAITED ALL THIS TIME JUST TO MAKE YOUR CONFESSION, MOTHER?
NO. I WAITED FOR THE CRUX.
AND NOW THE CRUX HAS COME.
THIS CAN END.
IT'S NOT NEEDED ANY LONGER.
YOU ALWAYS LET ME WALK AHEAD OF YOU. IS THIS DUTY OR CAUTION?
WHAT DO YOU THINK?
THAT IT DOESN'T MATTER. BECAUSE OUR PATHS PART VERY SOON.
YOU'RE LEAVING?
OH YES.
AND YOUR SERVANTS ARE DYING.
THEY WERE NEVER REALLY ALIVE.
THIS PLACE IS MORE LIKE A LIMB OR AN ORGAN THAN ANYTHING ELSE. OR A SEED, PERHAPS.
SEEDS DON'T DIE. THEY TRANSFORM INTO A DIFFERENT KIND OF LIFE.

MY DEAR LADY.
WHAT YOU MUST HAVE BEEN THROUGH!
WHAT IS THIS PLACE? AND WHO ARE YOU?
THIS PLACE IS BARROWJANE. OUR PIED-A-TERRE HERE IN THE SOFT PLACES.
I AM BERIM, OF THE JIN EN MOK. THIS IS SANDALPHON. AND THE SILK MAN YOU'VE ALREADY MET.
WE COME HERE FROM NUMEROUS MOMENTS, BOTH IN YOUR PAST AND IN YOUR FUTURE.
WE CAME TOGETHER BY CHANCE, INITIALLY-- BUT STAYED TO MEET YOU. TO THROW OURSELVES IN YOUR PATH, AS IT WERE.
WHY?
HA HA! WHY INDEED, WHY INDEED.
BECAUSE WE NEED YOU.
BECAUSE WE CAN DO NOTHING WITHOUT YOU.
BUT YOU MUST BE TIRED. PLEASE-- SIT DOWN.
I'LL HAVE TINA BRING REFRESHMENT.

THIS HOUSE-- WHAT IS IT MADE FROM? IT SEEMS TO BREATHE.
IT DOES BREATHE. THE BARROWJANE IS A LIVING ENTITY.
SHE HOUSES US AND FEEDS US, AND SLIVERS OF HER SUBSTANCE SERVE US.
BUT SHE'S OLD, AND HER ABILITY TO CAMOUFLAGE HERSELF HAS FALLEN OFF SOMEWHAT.
TEA AND CAKE, TINA.
SURE.
UMM... THE ANGEL LOOKS LIKE HE'S GONNA DIE. DID YOU WANT TO SPEAK TO HIM AGAIN?
HI I AM TINA
HMM. ACTUALLY, I SUPPOSE LILITH'S ARRIVAL MAKES HIM A LITTLE-- IRRELEVANT.
THEN LET'S BE RID OF HIM.
FOR SOME REASON THE PROXIMITY OF ANGELS MAKES ME THINK OF DEATH.
VERY WELL, THEN. I'LL DO IT.
I SAID I WOULD, AND I'M A MAN OF MY WORD.
I BELIEVE THAT YOU TOO, DEAR LADY, HAVE A CERTAIN ANIMUS AGAINST THE HOST OF HEAVEN.
I HATE THEM. I HATE THEM ALL, SAVE ONLY SAMAEL.
JUST SO. IN THAT CASE, I THINK YOU MAY ENJOY THIS.

I WON'T-- TELL YOU.
I WON'T TELL YOU ANYTHING.
WELL, IT'S AS LONG AS IT'S BROAD, OLD MAN.
WE HAVE SOMEONE ELSE ON THE JOB NOW.
SHE'S-- NOT AN ANGEL-- CAN'T-- HELP--
TRUE. VERY TRUE.
BUT SHE DOES KNOW THE STRUCTURE OF THE SILVER CITY.
GUUUH!
SHE BUILT IT, YOU SEE.

CUT HIM DOWN AND THROW HIM OUT, TINA.
YOU GOT IT.
AND CLEAN MY SPEAR, IF YOU'D BE SO KIND.
MY APOLOGIES. I SHOULD HAVE ASKED YOU IF YOU WANTED TO ADMINISTER THE COUP DE GRACE.
I DON'T TAKE ANY PLEASURE IN SLAUGHTER FOR ITS OWN SAKE.
AH. I DO, RATHER.
BUT THIS WAS NOT AS GRATUITOUS AS IT SEEMED.
IF HE'D LIVED, HE WOULD HAVE TRIED TO WARN THE HOST ABOUT OUR GRAND DESIGN.
AND WHAT'S THAT?
TO SMASH THE THRONE OF HEAVEN, RAPE AND MURDER ITS HOST OF ANGELS, AND CLOSE THE DOORS OF CREATION IN YAHWEH'S FACE.
SPEAKING OF WHICH, BY THE WAY--
--WE WERE HOPING TO ENLIST YOU

MOTHER, YOU'RE TALKING ABOUT THINGS THAT HAPPENED EONS AGO.
YES. I KNOW. BUT FOR ME, THAT WAS WHEN EVERYTHING CHANGED.
WHEN I CAME TO THE POINT OF DECISION, AND DECIDED.
THERE ARE TWO HORSES HERE. WHEREVER YOU'RE GOING, I'M NOT COMING WITH YOU.
BECAUSE THE MORNINGSTAR EXPECTS YOU?
YES.
BUT HE DOESN'T.
HE WENT TO THE ROOTS OF YGGDRASIL, AND HE NEVER CAME BACK.
KAROOOM

THE MORE REASON I HAVE TO GO TO HIM.
BUT BY THE TIME YOU WENT, YOU WOULDN'T FIND HIM THERE.
YOU SHOULD GO WITH ME, AND LEARN WHERE HE IS NOW.
IF YOU KNOW WHERE LUCIFER IS, THEN TELL ME.
MY PATIENCE IS ENDED.
WELL, I'D HOPED THAT FILIAL AFFECTION WOULD HAVE BROUGHT YOU A LITTLE FURTHER ALONG THE ROAD--
--BUT PERHAPS THIS WAY IS BEST, AFTER ALL.

LUCIFER'S COSMOS.
"MY DAUGHTER--
"--I HAVE SEEN THIS BEFORE, AND I KNOW WHERETO IT TENDS.
"IN ENDLESS ITERATION, LIKE WAVES AGAINST THE BASE OF A CLIFF.
"THE FUTURE, ERODING THE ROOTLESS ISLANDS OF OUR EXPERIENCE, MOMENT BY MOMENT.
"IT WILL END.
"EVERYTHING WILL END.
"BECAUSE OF OU EFFORTS, OR IN SPITE OF THEM.
"IT MATTERS NOT.
"I'VE SEEN IT
"IF I SEEM RUTHLESS NOW--
"--IT'S BECAUSE I'VE ALREADY MOURNED YOU."

MANY EONS AGO.
IF ANY PLACE SHOULD BE WATERED WITH TEARS, LADY LILITH--
--THEN IT SHOULD BE THIS--
--THE WORLD-TREE. WHICH IN TIMES TO COME, SOME WILL CALL YGGDRASIL.
AND WHICH IS ABOUT TO BE POISONED BY THE BLOOD OF THE ARCHANGEL MICHAEL.
CRUX
PART 2 OF 2
MIKE CAREY- WRITER
PETER GROSS & RYAN KELLY- ARTISTS
JARED K. FLETCHER- LETTERING
DANIEL VOZZO- COLORS AND SEPARATIONS
MICHAEL WM. KALUTA- COVER PAINTER
MARIAH HUEHNER-EDITOR
BASED ON CHARACTERS CREATED BY
GAIMAN, KIETH AND DRINGENBERG

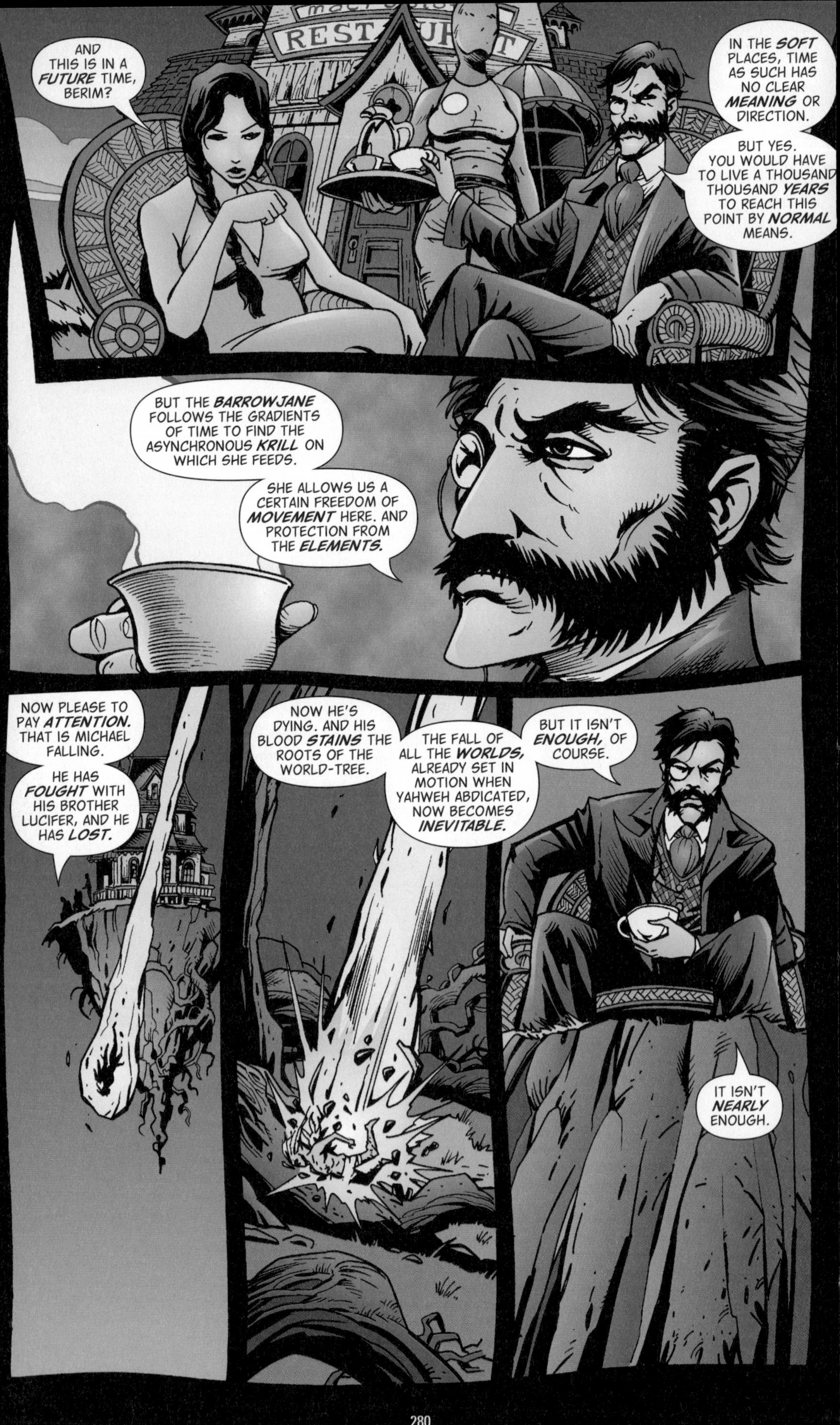
AND THIS IS IN A FUTURE TIME, BERIM?
IN THE SOFT PLACES, TIME AS SUCH HAS NO CLEAR MEANING OR DIRECTION.
BUT YES. YOU WOULD HAVE TO LIVE A THOUSAND THOUSAND YEARS TO REACH THIS POINT BY NORMAL MEANS.
BUT THE BARROWJANE FOLLOWS THE GRADIENTS OF TIME TO FIND THE ASYNCHRONOUS KRILL ON WHICH SHE FEEDS.
SHE ALLOWS US A CERTAIN FREEDOM OF MOVEMENT HERE. AND PROTECTION FROM THE ELEMENTS.
NOW PLEASE TO PAY ATTENTION. THAT IS MICHAEL FALLING.
HE HAS FOUGHT WITH HIS BROTHER LUCIFER, AND HE HAS LOST.
NOW HE'S DYING. AND HIS BLOOD STAINS THE ROOTS OF THE WORLD-TREE.
THE FALL OF ALL THE WORLDS, ALREADY SET IN MOTION WHEN YAHWEH ABDICATED, NOW BECOMES INEVITABLE.
BUT IT ISN'T ENOUGH, OF COURSE.
IT ISN'T NEARLY ENOUGH.

THERE IS A POWER WITHIN ME. THE DUNAMIS DEMIURGOS. GOD'S POWER.
WHEN I DIE, IT WILL POUR OUT OF ME AND OVERWHELM EVERYTHING THAT EXISTS.

I'M DYING NOW, ELAINE.
YOU HAVE TO TAKE THE POWER FROM ME.

TAKE IT-- TAKE IT FROM YOU?
SHE'S NOT STRONG ENOUGH. IT WILL DESTROY HER.
I CAN THINK OF NO OTHER WAY.

FATHER. OH GOD, I'M SORRY I NEVER CAME TO YOU. NEVER TRIED TO TALK--
IT WOULD HAVE DONE NO GOOD. I WAS PROUD, AND STUBBORN.
I COULD HAVE SOUGHT YOU OUT. I COULD HAVE--

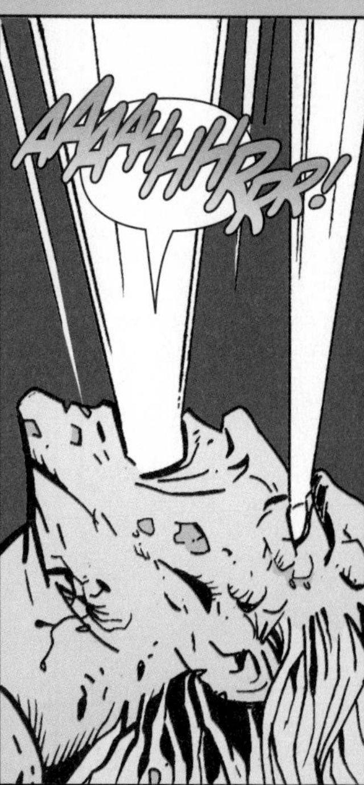

AAAAHHRRR!

OH GOD! OH GOD!
IT'S KILLING ME!
YES. SO I SEE.
THE POWER IS POURING INTO YOU. AND YOU'RE TOO SMALL.
IT NEEDS TO WELL UP FROM INSIDE YOU. THEN YOU'D HAVE SOME CHANCE OF SURVIVING IT.
FROM INSIDE? HOW-- HOW DO I--?
I HAVE NO IDEA. YOU'RE THE DEMIURGE.
PERHAPS IT COMES DOWN TO INSTINCT.

AND THAT'S THE LAST WE SEE OF THEM. BUT THEN WE'RE CLOSE TO THE POINT AT WHICH ALL THINGS END.
IT'S HARD EVEN FOR THE BARROWJANE TO SWIM AGAINST THESE CURRENTS.
WHY DID YOU SHOW ME THIS?
SO THAT YOU'D UNDERSTAND. IT IS A CHAIN-- A LOGICAL SEQUENCE.
GOD ABANDONS HIS THRONE, AND CREATION BEGINS TO CRUMBLE.
THEN FENRIS USES MICHAEL'S BLOOD TO ACCELERATE THE PROCESS.
AND SHOULD YAHWEH LIVE AND PROSPER WHILE THE WORLDS FALL?
ISN'T IT WORTH ANY COST TO MAKE HIM PAY FOR THIS?
YOU KNOW MY FEELINGS ON THAT. BUT WHAT WOULD THE COST BE?
YOUR CHILDREN.
WILL IT PLEASE YOU TO COME IN OUT OF THE COLD?

"'YOUR CHILDREN,' HE SAID. 'WILL IT PLEASE YOU TO COME IN OUT OF THE COLD?'
"BUT I NEVER COULD, OF COURSE.
"NOT SINCE THAT DAY."

ARE YOU SURE THAT THIS PART IS NECESSARY, BERIM?
YOU'VE SEEN IT.

SHE'S ONE OF THOSE WHO'D *OPPOSE* US.
AND *HER* VOICE WOULD BE LISTENED TO.
I KNOW. BUT I WISH I COULD *EXPLAIN* TO HER.
THAT THIS VENGEANCE IS AGAINST *YAHWEH* AND HIS ANGELS, NOT HER OR *LUCIFER.*
SHE'D *STILL* FIGHT YOU. SHE WOULDN'T *CARE* ABOUT YOUR REASONS.
"AND THAT WAS *TRUE,* OF COURSE.
"MY HATE WAS SO *PRIVATE,* IT COULDN'T BE TRANSLATED INTO ANY OTHER *LANGUAGE.*
"ALL I COULD DO NOW WAS SEE IT *OUT* TO ITS END.
"THE END I HAD BEEN SHOWN SO MANY YEARS *BEFORE.*"

"WHEN I SAW THE SHAPE OF THE FUTURE--
MY CHILDREN?
"--AND REALIZED IT HAD BOTH A BLADE AND A HILT."
I'VE EXPLAINED THIS. THEY'LL DIE IN ANY CASE. EVERYTHING WILL DIE.
BECAUSE YAHWEH WILL RENOUNCE HIS THRONE, AND LEAVE HIS CREATION TO DISINTEGRATE BEHIND HIM.
DEATH IS NOT MUCH. I MYSELF WILL ALREADY BE DEAD, LONG BEFORE THAT TIME.
TRUE, SILKMAN, AND OUR AIM IS A MODEST ONE. TO PUNISH YAHWEH FOR HIS CRUELTY AND INCOMPETENCE.
AND FOR THAT WE NEED THE LILIM.
TH-- THAT VIBRATION--
THE BARROWJANE IS DIVING AGAIN, INTO AN EARLIER AGE.
IT HURTS HER TO RISE TOO FAST.

EDEN GARDEN. WE'VE COME FROM THE *END* OF TIME TO ITS BEGINNING.

THERE *IS* NO BEGINNING. THIS OCEAN HAS NO *FLOOR.*

BUT WHEN YOU *LEAVE,* IT WOULD BE BEST IF YOU WERE *CLOSE* TO THE POINT AT WHICH YOU ENTERED.

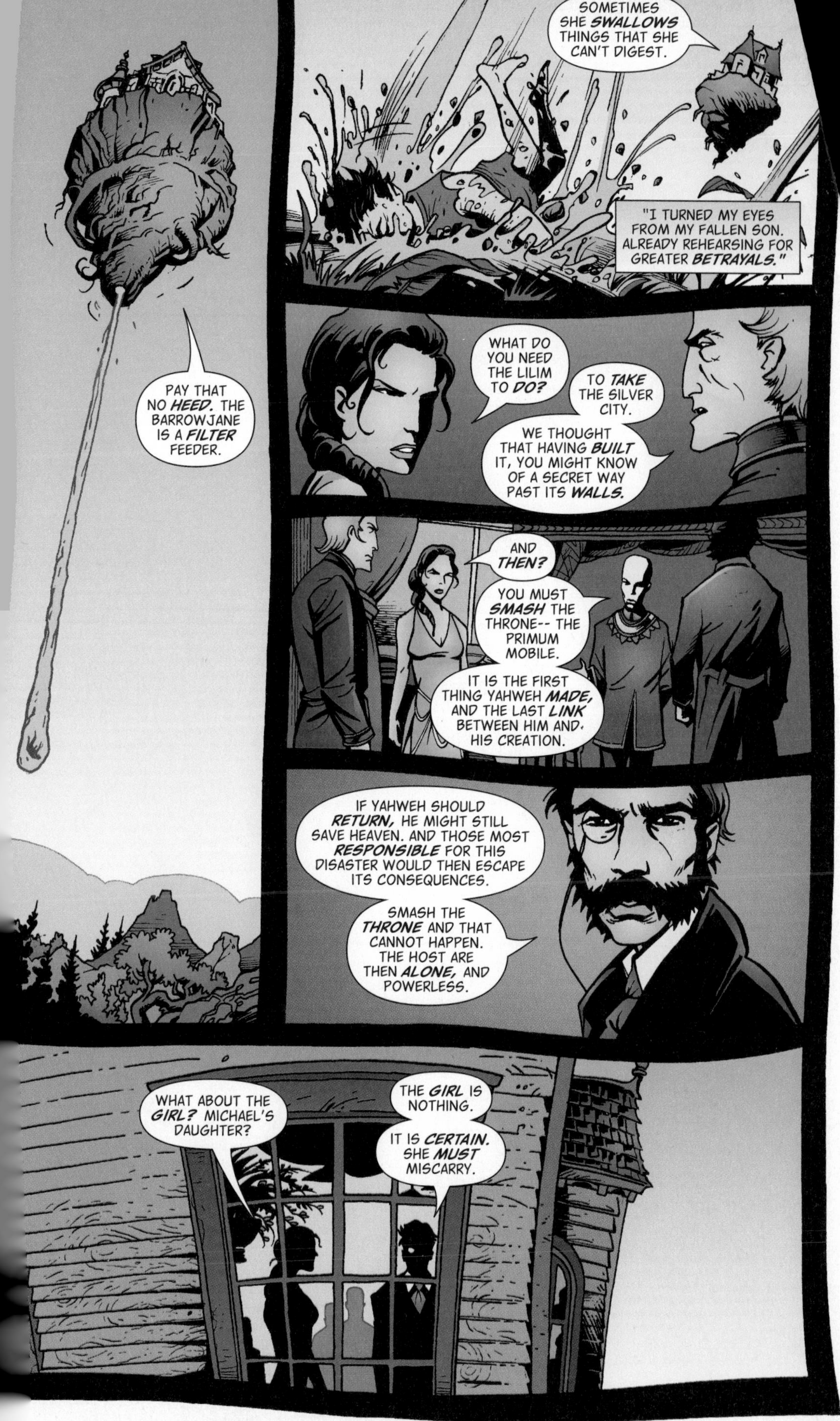
SOMETIMES SHE SWALLOWS THINGS THAT SHE CAN'T DIGEST.
"I TURNED MY EYES FROM MY FALLEN SON. ALREADY REHEARSING FOR GREATER BETRAYALS."
PAY THAT NO HEED. THE BARROWJANE IS A FILTER FEEDER.
WHAT DO YOU NEED THE LILIM TO DO?
TO TAKE THE SILVER CITY.
WE THOUGHT THAT HAVING BUILT IT, YOU MIGHT KNOW OF A SECRET WAY PAST ITS WALLS.
AND THEN?
YOU MUST SMASH THE THRONE-- THE PRIMUM MOBILE.
IT IS THE FIRST THING YAHWEH MADE, AND THE LAST LINK BETWEEN HIM AND HIS CREATION.
IF YAHWEH SHOULD RETURN, HE MIGHT STILL SAVE HEAVEN. AND THOSE MOST RESPONSIBLE FOR THIS DISASTER WOULD THEN ESCAPE ITS CONSEQUENCES.
SMASH THE THRONE AND THAT CANNOT HAPPEN. THE HOST ARE THEN ALONE, AND POWERLESS.
WHAT ABOUT THE GIRL? MICHAEL'S DAUGHTER?
THE GIRL IS NOTHING.
IT IS CERTAIN. SHE MUST MISCARRY.

"AND SHE IS TOO FRAIL A VESSEL.
"AS I SAID, WE HAVE NOT FOUND HER ON TIME'S FURTHER SHORE.
"SHE IS SWALLOWED BY THE POWER, AND SHE DOES NOT EMERGE AGAIN.
"WE BELIEVE SHE IS DISMANTLED BY IT.
"SHE IS, AFTER ALL, PARTLY OF HUMAN FLESH.
"AND IN THAT FURNACE, FLESH IS LIKE CHAFF IN A HURRICANE.
"WHAT COULD SHE HAVE TO SET AGAINST THAT WIND OF FIRE?
"HER WILL? HER HOPE? HER SMATTERING OF HALF-GLIMPSED WISDOM?
"NOTHING.
"SHE HAS NOTHING."

WELL, LADY? SPEAK. WILL YOU MAKE CAUSE WITH US?
WHAT CAUSE IS THAT?
DO YOU SEEK ANYTHING BEYOND DESTRUCTION?
DESTRUCTION IS A SINGLE BEAT OF THE ALL-ENCOMPASSING HEART.
THERE WILL BE OTHER CREATIONS. AND OTHER MAKERS, FAR MORE WORTHY.
IT'S TOO MUCH TO DO OUT OF HATRED. BUT THE CREATURES WHO DWELL IN THOSE OTHER CREATIONS--
--MIGHT THEY BECOME MORE THAN TOYS? MORE THAN PUPPETS ENACTING THEIR MAKER'S WILL?
IT IS TO BE HOPED.
THEN I'M YOURS.
WHEN THE CRUX COMES, I'LL LEAD MY CHILDREN AGAINST THE WALLS OF HEAVEN.
DEAR LADY, I'M DELIGHTED TO HEAR IT.
WE'LL ALL LEAVE SOON, AND GO BACK INTO THE WORLDS. I'M AFRAID THE WAIT WILL BE LONG.

BILIM CAMP.
"BUT THE FRUITION, WHEN IT FINALLY COMES--
"--ALL THE SWEETER FOR THAT."

WELL?
WILL NONE OF YOU WELCOME ME?

WILL NONE OF YOU GIVE ME THE HONOR THAT IS MY DUE?

WELCOME HOME.
MOTHER.
AH. HOME...
IS THAT WHAT THIS IS?

AND HAVE WE FALLEN SO FAR, MISRAN?
M--MOTHER?
I'VE WONDERED OFTEN HOW THINGS MIGHT HAVE GONE WITH YOU WHILE I WAS AWAY.
BUT THIS--
--THIS IS WORSE THAN MY WORST IMAGININGS.
I BADE YOU FIGHT FOR EDEN GARDEN, AND YOU'VE PITCHED YOUR TENTS IN A DESERT!
BRIADACH MADE MAZIKEEN OUR WAR LEADER. AND MAZIKEEN PLEDGED OUR SERVICE TO LUCIFER.
WE DECIDED--
DO THE LILIM SERVE?
DO THE LILIM EAT YAHWEH'S LEAVINGS? OR ADAM'S? NO.
THEN WHY SHOULD THEY EAT LUCIFER'S?

YOU HAVE FOLLOWED FALSE *PROPHETS.* FALSE *LEADERS.*
ONE OF THEM IS *THERE,* A BROKEN REED. BRING ME TO THE *OTHER.*

DO NOT *TOUCH* HER.

IT'S-- ONLY *WATER.* I THOUGHT SHE MIGHT BE--
DO NOT *APPROACH* HER.
LEST *HER* FATE FALL ALSO ON *YOU.*

BRIADACH.
MOTHER.
DID YOU SEE ME COMING?
I SEE THE SEED, AND I SEE THE ROT.
ROT IS WHAT YOU BRING. OF COURSE I SAW YOU COMING.
YOU HAVE BEEN THE STEWARD OF MY CHILDREN. AND YOU HAVE BETRAYED THEM.
AAAAAA!
BUT NOW THEIR TIME IS AT HAND.
NO. ONLY CHAOS IS AT HAND.
CHAOS, AND THEN A SILENCE THAT LASTS FOREVER.

I KNOW WHAT YOUR FRIENDS SHOWED YOU.
AND WHAT THEY FAILED TO SHOW YOU.
THERE WOULD HAVE BEEN A CHANCE FOR LIFE.
FOR THE WORLDS TO ENDURE.
BUT WHEN THE SILVER CITY FALLS, AND WHEN THE THRONE IS BROKEN, NOTHING THEN CAN--
KLUD
GAG HIM? MOTHER, IS THAT--?
IF HE SCREAMS. OR IF HE WAKES AND TRYS TO SPEAK WITH YOU...
TAKE HIM OUTSIDE, AND LAY HIM DOWN BESIDE HIS WICKED SISTER.
BIND HIS HANDS. AND IF HE SCREAMS, STOP HIS MOUTH.
A SACRIFICE SHOULD BE SOLEMN.
LET US TRY NOT TO MAR IT.

OH, THANK GOD!
IT'S STILL THERE!
LUCIFER, IT'S ALL STILL THERE!
THANK WHO?

THERE'S GROUND. AND SKY. EVERYTHING.
TO TOUCH. TO BREATHE.
YOU CAN'T AFFORD THEM, ELAINE.

I CAN'T--?
NO. KEEP IT SIMPLE. KEEP IT DOWN TO ONE THING.
NO REFRACTION OF THE LIGHT. NO MOVING PARTS.
BELIEVE ME, THIS IS HARDER THAN IT LOOKS.

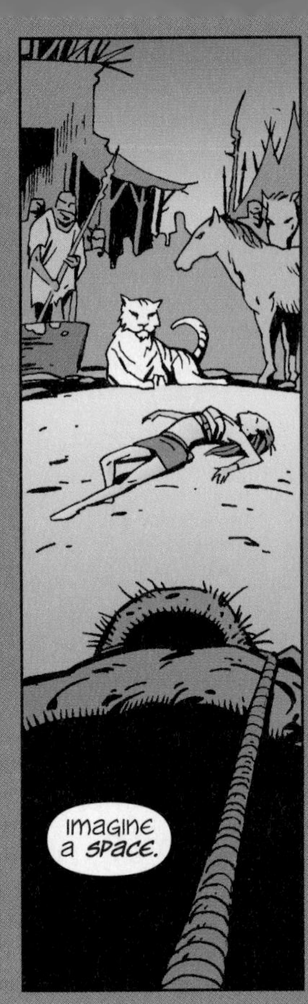
IMAGINE A SPACE.

THIS IS A SPACE. WHERE WE ARE. THIS IS--
THIS IS THE ABSENCE OF SPACE. PUSH AGAINST IT.

MAKE IT BACK AWAY FROM YOU. SO THAT YOU CAN FILL IT.

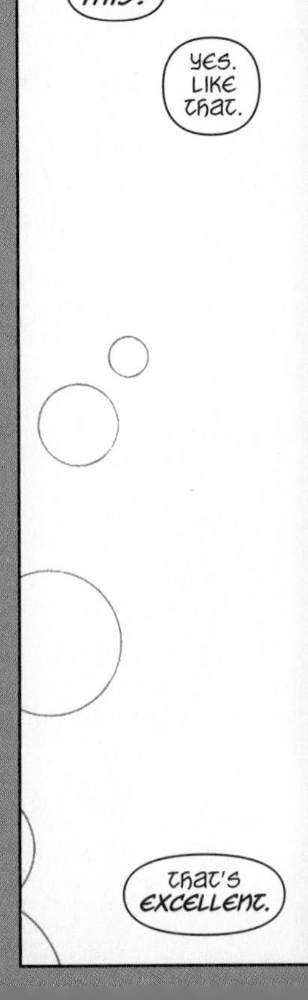
LIKE THIS?
YES. LIKE THAT.
THAT'S EXCELLENT.

NOW WE *BEGIN.*

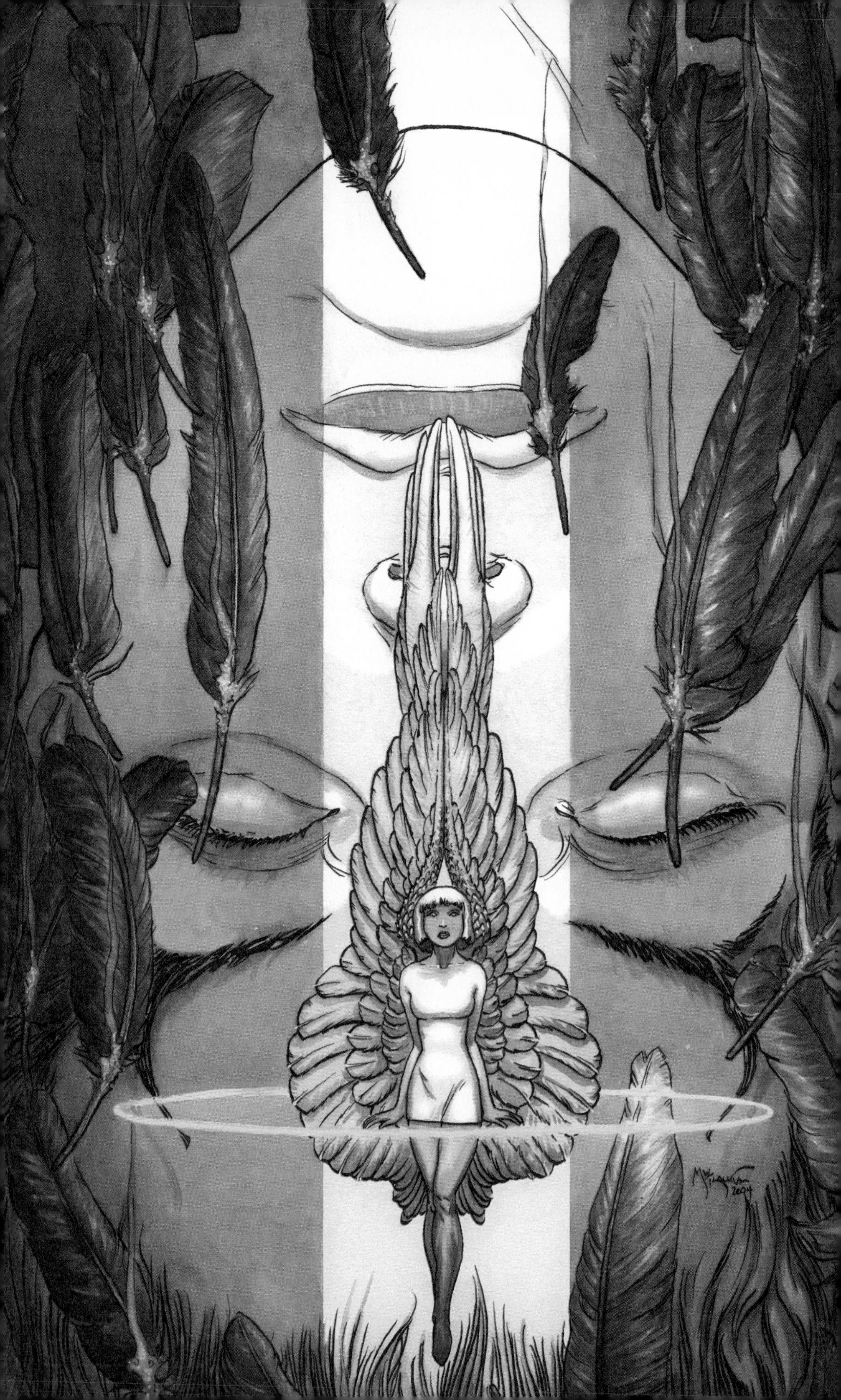

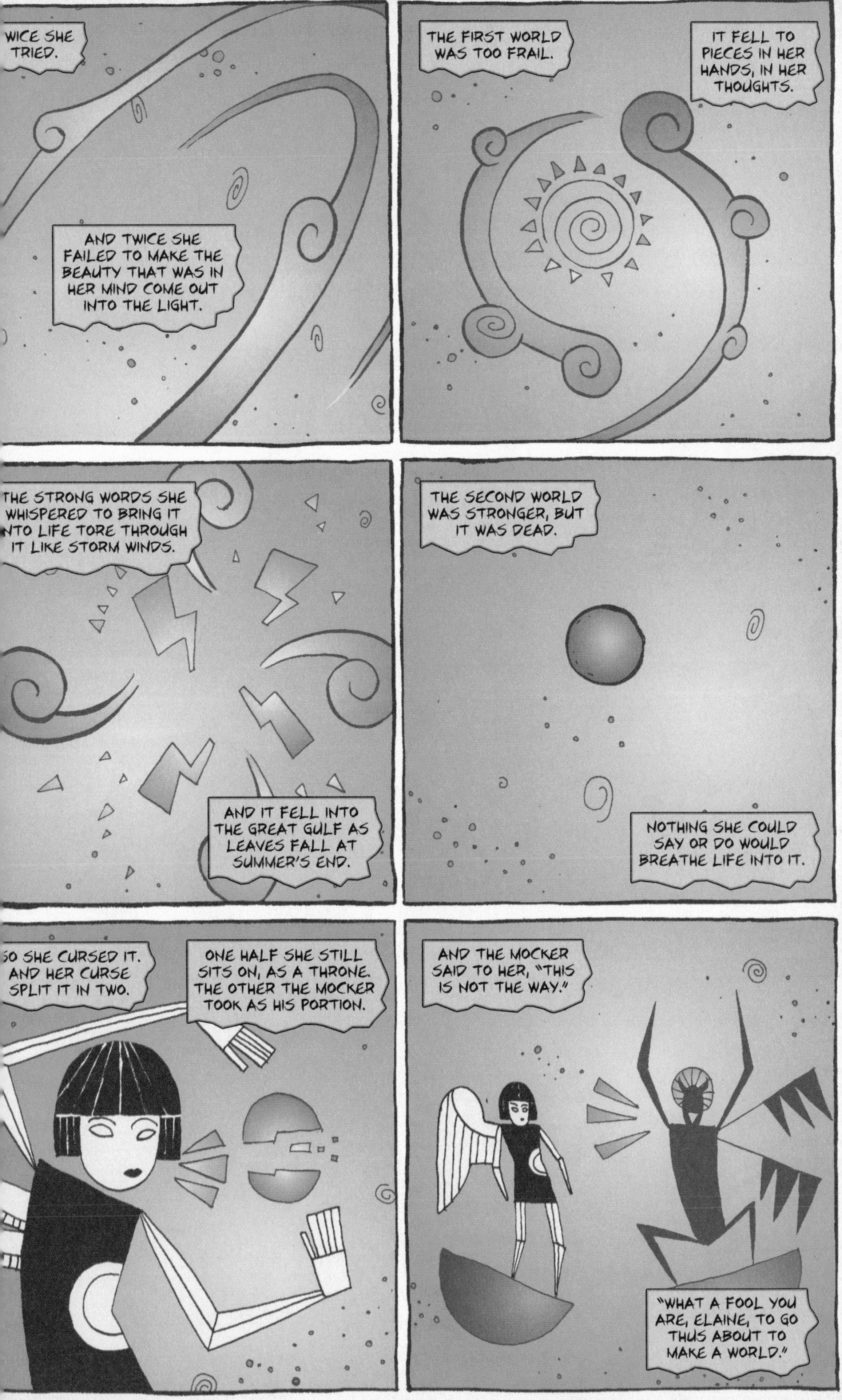

WICE SHE TRIED.
AND TWICE SHE FAILED TO MAKE THE BEAUTY THAT WAS IN HER MIND COME OUT INTO THE LIGHT.
THE FIRST WORLD WAS TOO FRAIL.
IT FELL TO PIECES IN HER HANDS, IN HER THOUGHTS.
THE STRONG WORDS SHE WHISPERED TO BRING IT NTO LIFE TORE THROUGH IT LIKE STORM WINDS.
AND IT FELL INTO THE GREAT GULF AS LEAVES FALL AT SUMMER'S END.
THE SECOND WORLD WAS STRONGER, BUT IT WAS DEAD.
NOTHING SHE COULD SAY OR DO WOULD BREATHE LIFE INTO IT.
O SHE CURSED IT. AND HER CURSE SPLIT IT IN TWO.
ONE HALF SHE STILL SITS ON, AS A THRONE. THE OTHER THE MOCKER TOOK AS HIS PORTION.
AND THE MOCKER SAID TO HER, "THIS IS NOT THE WAY."
"WHAT A FOOL YOU ARE, ELAINE, TO GO THUS ABOUT TO MAKE A WORLD."

IF YOU'RE SO CLEVER, LUCIFER, WHY AREN'T YOU DOING THIS?
IT'S NOT ME WHO NEEDS TO LEARN.
WHAT I NEED IS TO FIND A WAY OUT OF THIS STUPID PLACE.
THIS STUPID PLACE IS A UNIVERSE.
BUT I DIDN'T EVEN MEAN TO MAKE IT.
I KNOW. YOU WERE TRYING TO COPE WITH MICHAEL'S POWER WHEN HE DIED. TO DRAW IT OFF AND EARTH IT.
AND INSTEAD YOU DID THIS. YOU MADE A THIRD CREATION, TO STAND ALONGSIDE YAHWEH'S AND MY OWN.
BUT THAT DOESN'T MEAN WE HAVE TO SIT HERE AND PLAY GOD GAMES.
IF THE REAL UNIVERSE IS FALLING APART, WE SHOULD BE TRYING TO GET BACK THERE SO WE CAN HELP.
THE EXIT DOESN'T EXIST YET. WHEN IT DOES, WE'LL TAKE IT.
WELL, THANKS A LOT.
THAT'S JUST PERFECT.

AND THEN SHE SAID THE WORD PERFECT.
AND HEYA! THE THIRD WORLD-- THE PERFECT WORLD, WHERE WE LIVE NOW-- WAS BORN.
The Yahweh Dance
Writer Mike Carey Artist Ronald Wimberly
Colors Daniel Vozzo Letters Jared Fletcher
Cover Michael Wm. Kaluta Editor Mariah Huehner

BUT SHE LOOKED UPON THE EARTH, AND THERE WAS NOTHING TO LOOK BACK AT HER.
"THIS IS NOT GOOD," SHE SAID. "THIS IS NOT FIT. WHERE ARE THEY THAT SHALL KNOW ME?"
SO SHE RAN HER HAND THROUGH THE WATERS, AND THE WATERS TEEMED.
WHALE AND SHARK AND TURTLE AND RAY WERE BORN TO KNOW HER.
SHE LET HER SHADOW FALL ON THE LAND.
DEER AND CAT AND HORSE AND BADGER WERE BORN TO KNOW HER.
SHE BREATHED OUT HER BREATH INTO THE SKY.
EAGLE AND JAY AND PEACOCK WERE BORN TO KNOW HER.
AND LAST SHE MIXED HER SPIT WITH THE DIRT OF THE EARTH, AND SHAPED IT WITH HER FINGERS.
MAN WAS BORN TO KNOW HER.
BUT IN SPITE OF EVERYTHING THAT SHE HAD MADE--
--THE MOCKER STILL MOCKED, GIVING OUT SCORN AS A SNAKE GIVES POISON.

WHAT EXACTLY ARE YOU DOING?
MY BEST.
IT'S EASY FOR YOU TO SNEER. YOU'VE DONE THIS BEFORE.
AND I CAN'T EVEN SEE WHAT I'M DOING.
I HAVE TO SORT OF FEEL IT WITH MY MIND, AND THEN GUESS WHAT IT ALL MEANS.
LET ME REPHRASE THE QUESTION. WHAT ARE YOU DOING NOW?
IT WAS TOO COLD.
AND THE DECAY-- THING-- WHAT HAPPENS WHEN YOU DIE. THAT WASN'T WORKING RIGHT.
SO I'VE MADE THE CORE OF THE WORLD MOLTEN, TO RAISE THE SURFACE TEMPERATURE.
AND I'VE PUT IN SOME BUGS THAT EAT DEAD THINGS. DO YOU THINK THAT'LL DO IT?
SORRY.
THIS IS CALLED LEARNING BY DOING.

AND THE EARTH SHOOK.
AND THE HEAVENS RAINED FIRE.

"SURELY," THE PEOPLE SAID, "THE UNNAMED IS ANGRY WITH US, THAT HE SHAKES THE EARTH AND MAKES THE HEAVENS TO RAIN FIRE."
"LET US MAKE OUR PEACE WITH HIM."

AND THE COMELIEST WOMEN AND THE STRONGEST MEN CHOSE THEY FROM AMONGST THEM.
AND THESE THEY SANCTIFIED WITH PRAYERS AND BLESSINGS.

THEN THEY GAVE THEM TO THE FIRE, SAYING "THIS WE DO FOR HIM, THE UNNAMED, THAT HE WILL FAVOR US."

NO!
that's an activity that NEVER goes out of fashion.
IF you imagine you can STOP it, or even slow it down, you're going to be DISAPPOINTED.
IT'S GOING WRONG.
really? how?
THEY'RE KILLING EACH OTHER!
BUT THEY'RE DOING IT IN MY NAME.
they haven't GIVEN you a name.
I MEAN THEIR CREATOR'S NAME. IT COMES TO THE SAME THING.
OH TO HELL WITH THIS.
I'M GOING IN.

AND THEN IT WAS THAT SHE WALKED AMONG US.
SAYING "I AM SHE, THY MAKER, THY UNNAMED."
"BUT FROM THIS TIME FORTH YOU WILL CALL ME ELAINE."
"AND YOU WILL MAKE NO MORE SACRIFICES UNTO ME."
"I WILL NOT RECEIVE THEM, NOR THE PRAYERS THAT GO WITH THEM."
"BUT IF YOU PRAY WITH UNFEIGNED HEART, AND CONTRITE SPIRIT, THEN ONLY WILL I HEAR YOU."
"AND I WILL KEEP YOU SAFE."
"EVEN FOR LOVE OF YOU WHO ARE MY PEOPLE."

AND THOSE THAT WERE BY SAW THAT HER HAND, WHERE SHE DID QUENCH THE VOLCANO, WAS BLACK WITH SOOT.
THIS THEY TOOK TO BE A SIGN.
AND THEY SAID "WE WILL BE THE PEOPLE OF THE MARK."
"EVERY CHILD THAT IS BORN ALIVE AMONGST US, WE WILL INSCRIBE WITH THE MARK, TO SIGNIFY OUR COVENANT WITH ELAINE."
WHICH COVENANT ELAINE DID KEEP, AS SHE HAD PROMISED EREWHILE.
SO THAT THE PEOPLE OF THE MARK SPREAD THEIR DOMINION FROM THE MOUNTAINS TO THE SEA.
AND THEY MULTIPLIED, AND WAXED NUMEROUS.
UNTIL THEY DID COVER UP THE LAND.
UH OH.
AND STARVATION AND PLAGUE FELL UPON THEM.
AND BECAME THEIR NEMESIS.

IT'S THE BUGS. THE ONES I MADE TO BREAK DOWN THINGS THAT HAD DIED.
THEY'VE MUTATED, AND NOW THEY'RE KILLING PEOPLE!
SO?
SO I'LL MUTATE THEM BACK.
I SHOULD BE ABLE TO DO THAT WITHOUT--
...
BUT THEN THE POPULATION CRISIS WILL JUST GET WORSE.
THEY'LL STARVE, AND MURDER EACH OTHER FOR FOOD.
DO YOU HAVE A BETTER SOLUTION IN MIND?
I THINK--
I THINK MAYBE I'LL DO NOTHING.

In that time, one in three was taken. There were no hands to turn the plough, or work the pump.
Many there were that said Elaine had turned her face and her favor forever away from us.
But the assayers of the faith examined those that said so.
With patience and skill they shepherded the people of the mark back unto the paths of virtue.
And in due course Elaine smiled on her children again, as she was formerly wont to do.
They remembered the covenant, then, and went forth in great numbers to carry her word into distant lands-- lands of ice and fire and strange beasts.

In Terek Noi, to their amazement, they encountered a people who knew not Elaine--
--but worshipped instead an idol in the form of a great dog, which they called Arooon.
OH SHIIIIIIT!
The assayers of the faith took charge of their souls--
--and taught them of their grievous error.
HOW DID I MISS THAT? HOW COULD I MISS A WHOLE OTHER RACE?
I CAN'T DO THIS ANYMORE. I JUST CAN'T!
YOU HAVE TO DO IT.
TRUST ME.
THERE IS A POINT-- AND YOU'RE NEARLY THERE.

HWAET! IN FLOOD OF FLAME, AROOON FLEW DOWN FROM SKY HOUSE.
THE HEAT, THE HIDE, THE HAIR-- NO DOUBT HAD THEY THAT WITNESSED.
"I AM THY LORD," QUOD HE. "LISTEN, AND LEARN MY LORE."
"FEAR NOT THY FETTERS, AS FRAIL AS FALSE MEN'S FAITH."
CURSED ARE THESE CARLS THAT CLOG AND CUMBER THEE."
RISE FROM AMONG THEM. RUIN WILL I WREAK HERE."
"BUT IN MY PAW-PRINTS SHALT THOU PASS, PROTECTED."
"STRUCK STILL AS STONES, THESE STRANGERS SHALL NOT STAY THEE."
"SO GRIEVE NOT, FOR THY GOD IS NOW THY GUIDE."

"AND WITH FORTRESS WALLS WILL I FOLD THEE FAST."
"HIGH UNTO HEAVEN HEAVE THE TREES, TO HIDE THEE."
"THAT MAN MAY NOT MAR OR MELL WITH THEM THAT ARE MINE."
AND IF *THAT* DOESN'T WORK, I'M GIVING *UP*.

And the Great Wall stood.
For a thousand years, or perhaps a little longer.
On the Northern side of it, monsoons fell perpetually, year after year.
While to the South, there was eternal drought.
A land of fire where nothing could grow.
That's what I heard, anyway.
What's your version?
PRETTY MUCH THE SAME AS *YOURS,* ESPEDON.
EXCEPT THAT AROOON WAS A *WOLF* GOD. AND YOUR *ELAINE* I NEVER HEARD OF.
It doesn't matter. We're pretty much a secular society now.
Nobody actually believes in her anymore.
WELL *SOMETHING* BUILT THE WALL, AND IT SURE WASN'T US.
YOU KNOW, THIS CONVERSATION WOULD GO A LOT *QUICKER* IF YOU COULD ASTRAL-*PROJECT.*

Yeah, well I can't. I have to physically see my words to send them into your head.
But I'm a shit-hot psychic lens. And that's what I'm here for.
HEY, YOU'RE HERE TO DIE, SOUTHERN BOY. SAME AS THE REST OF US.
You don't have to look so dam cheerful about
YOU'RE NOT HAPPY? I'M VERY HAPPY.
THIS IS WHERE WE GET TO SMACK THE FACE OF GOD.
NO MORE WALLS. NO MORE QUAKING IN FEAR AT THE EYE IN THE SKY.
THAT'S A GOOD THING TO DIE FOR, ESPEDON.
Yes. It is.
Goodbye, Quadmin. I wish I could have spoken to you just once, face to face.
And I wish that our bodies could have touched as our spirits have done.

ARE WE ALL MET, TREMOIL?
AYE, SIR. AND ALL READY.
WILL YOU SPEAK TO THEM?
WELL, I WAS GOING TO GIVE A SPEECH OF A SINGLE WORD. "NOW!"
BUT WHY NOT? CERTAINLY MY ORATORY SHOULD PUT THEM IN THE RIGHT MOOD FOR SUICIDE.

MY FRIENDS, YOU HAVE ***COME*** HERE TO TAKE PART IN A GREAT ***VENTURE.***

TO ***KILL*** YOURSELVES-- AND AS YOU DIE, TO THROW THE ***PAIN*** OF YOUR DEATHS AGAINST THE WALL.

A HUNDRED ***THOUSAND*** MORTAL WOUNDS ARE A GREAT FORCE ***INDEED.***

AND I-- YOUR ***LENS--*** WILL MAGNIFY THEM SO THAT THEY ARE EVEN ***GREATER.***

BUT STILL, THE WALL ***MIGHT*** ENDURE.

WERE IT NOT FOR THE ***NORTHERLINGS--*** OUR ANCIENT ENEMIES. THEY TOO HAVE CHOSEN A HUNDRED THOUSAND TO ***DIE,*** AND A LENS TO ***FOCUS*** THE DEATHS.

THIS, WE HOPE, WILL BE ***ENOUGH.***

TCHANG
TCHANG
TCHANG
TCHANG
OKAY.
YOU'VE *MADE* YOUR POINT.
I'LL TAKE THE WALL DOWN NOW.

THAT LOOKS LIKE *SURRENDER.*
I DON'T *CARE* WHAT IT LOOKS LIKE.
AND I DON'T WANT TO HEAR ANY MORE FROM *YOU* ABOUT IT.
THAT SOUNDS *PROMISING.*
GO *ON.*
GO ON AND *WHAT?* DRAW THE *MORAL?*
THAT THE LIFE OF *PUPPETS* IS NO LIFE AT ALL?
YOU KNEW THAT *ALREADY.* AND IT ISN'T EVEN THE *POINT.*
YOU JUST WANTED ME TO DO THE *GOD* THING. THE *YAHWEH* DANCE.
SO I'D GET USED TO USING THE *POWER.* SO I'D GET THE *FEEL* OF IT.

ALL RIGHT.
THIS IS PROBABLY GOING TO LOOK A BIT RAGGED AROUND THE EDGES.
ELA
INE
LOS

And then she left us.

To rejoin some great struggle of gods and monsters left unfinished elsewhere.

SO I GO BACK TO THE *CITY.*

TO TELL THE DEVIL I NEED TO GET *FIXED.*

YEEEHAAA!

FIVE IF THEY BLEED! TEN IF THEY FALL DOWN!

GAME ON!

The BREACH

part 1 of 3

MIKE CAREY writer
PETER GROSS & RYAN KELLY artists
ARED K. FLETCHER lettering
DANIEL VOZZO colors and separations
MICHAEL W. KALUTA cover painter
MARIAH HUEHNER editor

FIVE EACH! I SLOWED HER DOWN.
TEN!
UKKK!

TEN EACH.
NO ONE SAID THEY COULDN'T FALL DOWN TWICE.

HEY.
HOW MUCH DOES THIS COUNT FOR?

CRUNCHHH
GAAAHH!

BITCH! FUCKING BITCH! JOHN, GET THE KEROSENE.
PITCH IT OVER HER!

I'M TAKING THIS IN STRIDE, YOU UNDERSTAND.
THE THING THAT'S INSIDE ME-- MUCH AS I HATE IT-- HAS ITS OWN WAYS OF PROTECTING ITSELF.

YOU'D BETTER NOT DO THIS. REALLY.
TCHAH! THANKS FOR THE ADVICE.
BUT IT'S A NICE FUCKING NIGHT FOR A BARBECUE.

AH! AH! AAAAHH!
WELL, THERE YOU GO.
I TRIED TO WARN YOU.

OH GOD!
OH GOD!

SSSSSSSSS

THAT'S ALL IT TAKES, REALLY.
WHATEVER KIND OF CRAZY THEY ARE, THEY STILL KNOW TO BE SCARED.

BUT THE DAMAGE IS ALREADY DONE.
ARE YOU ALL RIGHT?
I-- HHHHH--
--I DON'T THINK SO.

NO. I DON'T THINK SO EITHER.
IS THERE ANYONE-- YOU KNOW-- WHO I SHOULD CALL?

IT DOESN'T MATTER. THIS-- THIS IS JUST A SIGN.
A *SIGN?*
A SYMPTOM. THE WORLD IS-- UNRAVELING-- AND IT'S GOING TO GET A LOT WORSE.
LISTEN. LISTEN TO ME.
YOU HAVE TO GO TO VEGAS AGAIN. TO THE-- FIORENZE.
DEAD BIRDS. AND A MAN SAYING "SPIN IT-- SPIN IT, KID."
THIRTEEN *BLACK* WILL WIN.
BET *EVERYTHING.*
EVERYTHING YOU HAVE--
"NOW YOU SEE THEM AS THEY *ARE.*
"AS WE *ALL* WILL BE, IN THE END."

STRIPPED OF THEIR DISGUISES.
IN THE OPEN, WITH NOWHERE TO HIDE.
I CANNOT SAY, MY DEAR ONES, HOW IT HURTS ME TO SEE THIS. THESE FALSE PROPHETS PLAYING ON YOUR FAITH.
WHILE THEY SELL YOU IN SERVITUDE TO THE MORNINGSTAR.
BUT-- MAZIKEEN IS OUR SISTER, AND BRIADACH OUR BROTHER.
WHATEVER THEY'VE DONE, MOTHER, IS KINSHIP NOT STRONGER THAN ANGER?
KINSHIP IS WHAT THEY BETRAYED WHEN THEY LIED TO YOU.
KINSHIP IS WHAT CRIES OUT FOR VENGEANCE NOW. THOUGH YOU WEEP FOR IT. THOUGH WE ALL WEEP FOR IT.

WHAT SHALL BE DONE WITH THEM, MOTHER?
HOW WILL WE PUNISH THEM?
THEY WILL RUN THE GAUNTLET-- RECEIVING ONE BLOW FROM EACH OF YOU.
BECAUSE THEY HAVE INJURED EACH OF YOU.
AFTER THAT, YOU MAY DIG A PIT AND BURY THEM.
PUT THEM AND ALL THEIR BASE COUNSEL OUT OF YOUR SIGHT AND YOUR MINDS FOREVER.
SEE, MOTHER HERE IS ONE MORE TO BE JUDGED.
A HUMAN WOMAN, WHO MAZIKEEN BROUGHT HERE TO BE HER WHORE.
IF I NEEDED ANY FURTHER PROOF OF BETRAYAL, I SEE IT HERE.
TO TAKE A DAUGHTER OF EVE INTO HER BED. TO CONSORT SO OPENLY WITH OUR ENEMIES!

YOU THINK YOU'VE *BEATEN* HER.
NOBODY BEATS HER. SHE'LL *KILL* YOU.
GIVE HER A SKIN OF *WATER,* AND TURN HER *OUT* INTO THE WASTES.
SHE HAS NO *BUSINESS* HERE.
BYE BYE.
BEATRICE.
SKRRRT

THE STRIP. FIRST PACIFIC BANK.
ONE BLOCK UP FROM THE FIORENZE.
SURE.
HOPE YOUR REENTRY IS SMOOTHER THAN YOUR TAKEOFF.
HOPE SPRINGS ETERNAL, LADY.
'LEAST, THAT'S WHAT I HEARD.
DOESN'T MEAN IT'LL GET YOU WHERE YOU'RE GOING.
KLIK

--ECHOES THE FINDINGS OF THE HOWARD LEAGUE **PRISON** CHARITY, WHICH REPORTS AN EIGHT HUNDRED PER CENT **INCREASE** IN PRISONER SUICIDES ACROSS THE U.S..

I DON'T SUPPOSE YOU FEEL LIKE SWITCHING TO A ***MUSIC*** CHANNEL.

I DON'T ***SUPPOSE.***

IN THE POPULATION AT **LARGE,** THOUGH, THE FIGURE IS CONFUSED BY ACTS OF **SELF-MUTILATION** WHICH RESULT IN ACCIDENTAL DEATH. HERE, TOO, INCIDENCE IS RISING BY--

OR SPICS

KEE VEG PURE

NO BLACKS OR SPICS

ARE YOU SURE YOU WANT TO TAKE ALL OF THIS IN *CASH,* MISS PRESTO?

I WIRED *AHEAD.* I WAS TOLD THERE WOULDN'T BE ANY *PROBLEM.*

NO, NO. NO PROBLEM. IT'S JUST-- WELL, THE *AMOUNT--* THE RISK OF--

I'LL BE *FINE.* THANKS.

THAT'S HIM.

RIGHT *THERE.*

"HE IS TRAMPLING
OUT THE VINTAGE.
HYAAAAA!
"HE IS PRESSING WINE
FROM OUT OF THE
GRAPES OF WRATH--
"--SO THAT THE
LAST CUP MAY BE
POURED, AND
OFFERED TO US."

OH MOTHER, YOU HAVE DINED AND SUPPED ON *MADNESS.*
ON *REVELATION.*
AS YOU *WILL.*
BUT WHAT *YOU* SAW WAS ONLY *ONE* EPIPHANY.
THE PAST AND THE FUTURE ARE THE AIR I *BREATHE,* AND I HAVE *SEEN* WHERE THIS GOES.
YOU WILL DESTROY *EVERYTHING.* BUT EVERYTHING IS *NOTHING.*
AND YOU WILL BE THE *QUEEN* OF NOTHING, WHEN THERE IS NOTHING ELSE *LEFT* FOR YOU TO BE.
YOU WILL *LIVE* TO SEE--
GWUUUUH!
ON WITH THE *WORK.*
BEFORE THE *LIGHT* STARTS TO FAIL YOU.

THE FIORENZE. GETTING A LITTLE LATE, NOW. OR AT LEAST THAT'S HOW IT FEELS.
BUT IN VEGAS YOU'RE NEVER GONNA SEE A CLOCK.
MAKE ROOM FOR THE LADY.
HELL, I WAS LEAVING ANYWAY.
THANK YOU.
THERE YOU GO, MISSY.
HOPE YOUR LUCK IS BETTER THAN MINE.
I'M LOOKING TO CHANGE IT.

SPLATCH
THWUCK
SPLATCH
SPLATCH
THWUCK
THWUCK
NEVER MIND THAT. JUST SPIN THE WHEEL, KID.
SOME OF US CAME HERE TO PLAY.
ALL OF IT.
ALL OF IT ON RED.

TABLE'S CLOSED, LADIES AND GENTLE-MEN.
RIEN NE VA PLUS. NO MORE BETS.
TUNK
TUNK
13
THIRTEEN.
BLACK.
JESUS! HARD LINES, LADY.
EASY COME.
EASY GO.

HELL OF A STORM.
YEAH.
THOUGHT I KNEW THE CITY PRETTY WELL, BUT SHIT! I NEVER SAW HER LIKE THIS BEFORE.

NEVER SAW A PLAY LIKE YOURS BEFORE, EITHER.
BETTING A STACK LIKE THAT, KNOWING YOU WERE GONNA LOSE...

UNLESS-- AND I COULD BE OUT OF *LINE* HERE-- YOU'RE BETTING ON SOMETHING *ELSE.*
LIKE WHAT?
LIKE I *DUNNO.*
LIKE MAYBE-- THAT ANY GODS WHO LIVE ROUND *HERE* WOULD SOONER HAVE A BIG ROLL ON THE *WHEEL* THAN A FATTED CALF.
IF YOU WERE GONNA MAKE 'EM AN *OFFERING,* I MEAN.
DKNY

HELL OF A STORM.

LIGHTNING! OUT OF A CLEAR SKY. THE MORNINGSTAR--
THE MORNINGSTAR IS PASSED OUT OF THE SCHEME OF THINGS.
CARRY ON WITH YOUR WORK.
BUT MOTHER, WE CAN'T.
LOOK! LOOK THERE!
SHE'S GONE.
MAZIKEEN IS GONE.

VIVA LAS VEGAS.
THE PLACE THAT GREW FROM A HUMBLE MIRAGE INTO A GLORIOUS, CITY-SIZED CON TRICK.
EVEN THE NAME IS A SCAM. YOU SEE ANY MEADOWS HERE? NO, ME NEITHER.
BUT TONIGHT, WITH THE SKY TRYING TO BLOW IT AWAY AND THE DESERT TRYING TO SWALLOW IT WHOLE, IT FEELS LIKE YOU'D ONLY HAVE TO RUB YOUR EYES AND IT WOULD VANISH--
--TO THE TEPID APPLAUSE OF ITS JADED CLIENTELE.
The BREACH
part 2 of 3
MIKE CAREY writer
PETER GROSS & RYAN KELLY artists
ARED K. FLETCHER lettering
DANIEL VOZZO colors
ICHAEL WM. KALUTA cover painter
ARIAH HUEHNER editor
ased on characters created by
GAIMAN, KIETH, DRINGENBERG

SO YOU COME TO US.
YOU COME TO US WITH A PROPOSITION, IF I MAY PUT IT IN SUCH A WAY.
SAYS THE GANGSTER GHOST GOD THING.
YOU GOT YOURSELF IN TROUBLE. NOW YOU WANNA GET YOURSELF FIXED. VEGAS UNDER-STANDS THAT, BUT STILL--
OPINION IS KIND OF DIVIDED.
DIVIDED? WHAT THE FUCK DOES THAT MEAN?
IF I MAY PUT IT IN SUCH A WAY.
THERE'S THE OLD FIGHTING SPIRIT, JILLY GIRL. ONLY YOU DON'T WANNA GO FIGHTING ME, 'CAUSE I'M YOUR FRIEND.
MY FRIEND?
SURE. I'M ON YOUR SIDE. I GOT MONEY ON YOU, IN A SENSE.
LET'S TAKE A WALK.
ASSUMING YOU GOT NOTHING BETTER TO DO.

KAROOM
LOOKS LIKE THE END OF THE WORLD, N'T IT? A STORM THAT TRETCHES ACROSS ALL HE FUCKING REALMS. NICE EFFECT...
"DIVIDED"?
YEAH, I WAS COMING TO THAT.
OPLESS GIRLS OF
SENSATIONAL
VEGAS APPRECIATES THE OFFERING YOU MADE. AND HOW YOU MADE IT.
BUT VEGAS ALSO LIKES THE THING THAT'S INSIDE YOU. THE THING THAT SHUFFLES DESTINIES LIKE CARDS.
VERY MUCH, VEGAS LIKES THAT.
HENCE MY PREVIOUS REMARK. VEGAS IS, YOU COULD SAY, OF TWO MINDS ABOUT THIS.
SO WILL YOU HELP ME?
YES OR NO, BECAUSE I DON'T HAVE TIME FOR THIS BULLSHIT.
YES AND NO, IS MORE OR LESS WHAT WE DECIDED. HERE, YOU WANT ONE OF THESE CUBANAS?
I FEEL LIKE I'M ABOUT TO HAVE A KID OF MY OWN.

LUCIFER'S CREATION.

THE ARMED CAMP OF THE *LILIM.*

HAAAAAAH!

DO YOU STILL BELIEVE YOU CAN *DO* THIS, BERIM?

I-- *HAVE--* DONE IT.

LOOK-- *OUTSIDE* AND SEE.

THE GATES WERE TRYING TO *OPEN,* LILITH, TO *CONNECT* TO THIS TIME, AND THIS PLACE.

BUT I HELD THEM *OFF.* AGAIN.

HOW DO YOU KNOW THEY'RE LUCIFER'S GATES?
THEY BORE SOME-ONE *ELSE'S* NAME.
ELAINE. ELAINE *BELLOC.*

MICHAEL'S DAUGHTER.
MICHAEL'S--?
YES. WE *MISCALCULATED.*

THEN WE'LL *FAIL!* ALL OUR PLANS WILL *MISCARRY...*
THEY *DIDN'T* DIE. THEY WENT SOMEWHERE *ELSE,* WHERE WE COULDN'T SEE.
HARD TO *IMAGINE* WHERE SUCH A SOMEWHERE MIGHT *BE.*

NO. AS I SAID, I'VE *DELAYED* THEM. HEADED THEM OFF.
THIS *CONTINUES* TO BE A MATTER OF TIME.

AND TIME FAVORS *US.*

TOK

IT'S DONE.

WE'VE NOT TAMPED THE **EARTH** DOWN. OR MADE IT--

I SAID IT'S **DONE.**

IVRIMEL? PASS ME THE MATTOCK, THERE!
THIS IS BUT FOOL'S WORK WITH THE BACK OF A SHOVEL.
KKKHHHH!
KRAKK
WHERE IS THE SOT?
LET'S DRAG HIM AWAY BY HIS HEELS.
BEFORE WE CHOKE ON THIS BLOODY DUST.

COME ON, SCRATCHPOLL.
LET'S GET IN OUT OF THIS, AND DRINK A--

KRAKSH
M--MAZIKEEN! NO!
WE DIDN'T CHOOSE THIS! IT'S NOT-- IT'S NOT--
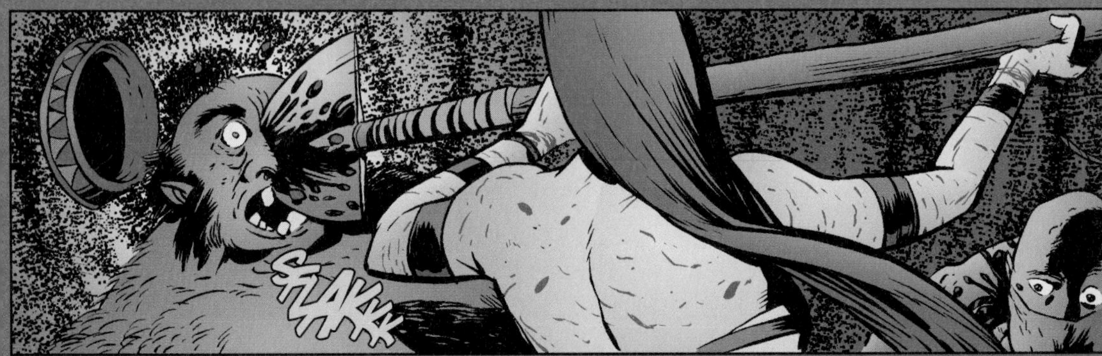
SHLAKKK

GLKKK

BLOOD FOR BLOOD, BROTHER.
AND MORE TO COME.

WE WALK TO THE EDGE OF TOWN.
NOT HARD TO DO, IN VEGAS. ANY STREET YOU LOOK DOWN, THE DESERT'S THERE.
WAITING FOR ITS MOMENT.
THREE HUNDRED MILES OF NOTHING, BETWEEN HERE AND GRANTS.
CLEAR ACROSS ARIZONA INTO NEW MEXICO. THAT'S WHERE YOU'RE GOING.
YOU SEE THAT?
THERE'S NOTHING THERE TO SEE.
WELL, NOTHING'S WHAT I'M TALKIN' ABOUT.
YOU THINK SO?
YEAH, I THINK SO. BECAUSE IT'S THE ONLY SHOT IN YOUR LOCKER, MISSY.
VEGAS HAS SPOKEN. AND IT'S NOT KNOWN FOR GIVING ANYONE AN EVEN BREAK.
WE WANT THIS BIRTH TO GO AHEAD. BUT WE'RE GIVING YOU A CHANCE TO SQUARE IT WITH THE KID BEFORE IT COMES OUT O' YOU.
Y'KNOW, SO IT DON'T COME OUT FIGHTING.

IT'S THEIRS. IT'S WHAT'S LEFT OF THEM. THE BASANOS.
THEY FUCKING ENSLAVED ME! THEY RODE ME LIKE A HORSE! YOU THINK I WANT TO GO BACK TO THAT?
NO. I DON'T GUESS YOU WOULD.
BUT THIS IS THE DEAL. SO YOU GET THE FINGERS OFF THE FABRIC, MAKE LIKE A GOOD GIRL--
--AND I'LL GIVE YOU THE STARTING PRICES.
OW! SHIT, OKAY.
GOOD. THANK YOU. SO YOU'RE GONNA GO THAT WAY, WHICH IS DUE EAST.
SOMEONE'S WAITING FOR YOU ON THE OTHER SIDE. BUT YOU DON'T EAT. YOU DON'T DRINK. AND YOU GOTTA MAKE IT BEFORE THE SUN COMES UP.
THREE HUNDRED MILES IN ONE NIGHT? HOW CAN ANYONE DO THAT?
BY CHEATING, I GUESS. GONNA BE INTERESTING TO WATCH, EITHER WAY.
SEE YOU IN THE FUNNY PAPERS.

THERE'S ONLY ONE HORSE MISSING. AND ONE SET OF PRINTS.
MAZIKEEN.
OF COURSE.
SHE IS AN IMPONDERABLE, LILITH. SHE KNOWS THAT YOU'RE CENTRAL TO OUR PLANS.
THAT ALONE WOULD TELL THE MORNINGSTAR TOO MUCH, IF SHE WERE TO ENCOUNTER HIM.
I'LL ASSEMBLE SEARCH PARTIES, AND LEAD THEM MYSELF.
WE CAN RUN HER DOWN BEFORE SHE GOES TOO FAR.
WITH RESPECT, NO.
NOW IS WHEN YOU MUST BIND YOUR CHILDREN TO OUR CAUSE.
ALL MUST HEAR YOU, AND ALL MUST SWEAR TO YOU. THERE'S NO OTHER WAY.

YOU'VE ALSO GOT TO BE HERE TO GREET OUR ALLIES, WHEN THEY COME-- SINCE THEY'LL ONLY ANSWER TO YOU.
SO I WILL DEAL WITH MAZIKEEN.
AND WHEN SHE'S DEAD, I'LL RETURN TO YOU.
VERY WELL, BERIM. BUT BE WARY.
LET MY ENEMIES BE WARY.
I WILL BE SUDDEN.
AND THOROUGH.

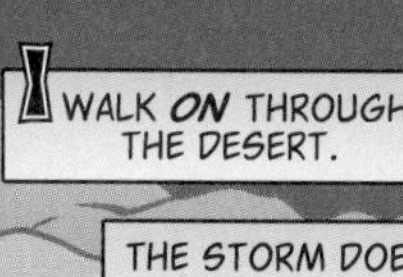
I WALK ON THROUGH THE DESERT.

THE STORM DOESN'T TOUCH ME. IT'S NOT ALLOWED TO.
BUT I WONDER WHAT TIME IT IS, AND HOW LONG I'VE GOT.

THEN THE WIND DIES, AND THE MOON COMES UP.
AND I'VE GOT AT LEAST A ROUGH IDEA.

YOU THINK OF THE DESERT AS A HOT PLACE, BUT IT'S GOT A DIFFERENT FACE THAT IT WEARS AT NIGHT.
AFTER A WHILE, THE COLD STARTS TO SEEP RIGHT THROUGH ME.

FIGURES. I CAN'T BE HURT. THE MONSTER INSIDE ME WILL MAKE SURE OF THAT.
BUT THE COLD WILL SLOW ME DOWN-- WHICH IS WHAT IT WANTS.

"YOU DON'T EAT."
"YOU DON'T DRINK."

Flamingo
LOS VEGAS
YOU KNOW--
--HE DIDN'T SAY A WORD ABOUT NOT SMOKING.

HEYA, PRETTY BIRD.
MAY I SHARE YOUR FIRE THIS COLD, COLD NIGHT?
UMM-- THAT'D BE GREAT. IF I HAD ONE.
BUT I SAW YOU MAKE A FIRE, WITH YOUR MAGIC.
LOOK BEHIND YOU.

IT IS GOOD TO SHARE HEAT ON A NIGHT LIKE THIS.
YEAH. I SUPPOSE.
AND THIS IS A VERY GOOD FIRE. IF THE SMOKE DOESN'T MAKE YOU TOO DROWSY.
BUT BETTER IS TO SHARE THE BODY'S HEAT.
MY LOINS AS I LOOK AT YOU ARE HOTTER THAN ANY FIRE.
MMMMM.
MMMPH?
HEY, WHAT IS THIS?
YOU WERE A DOG A MINUTE AGO! NOW YOU'RE COMING ON TO ME?
I WAS A COYOTE. I STILL AM, THOUGH I WEAR A MAN'S SKIN.
BUT IN ANY SHAPE, MY SEED IS STRONG.

YOU KNOW HOW THE COWBIRD THROWS OTHER CHICKS OUT OF THEIR OWN NEST?
EVEN SO, MY SEED THROWS OUT OTHER MEN'S SEED. FUCK WITH ME, AND YOU WILL BEAR MY CHILDREN ONLY.
YOU KNOW, THAT'S A GREAT LINE. IF YOU KEEP TRYING, YOU'RE BOUND TO FIND SOME GIRL WHO'LL FALL FOR IT.
THEN YOU REFUSE ME?
OH YEAH.

EVEN THOUGH I DANCED A CHARM AROUND YOU, TO MAKE YOU DESIRE ME.
THE GAMBLER SAID THAT YOU WERE CLEVER.

VERY WELL. I COULD FORCE YOU--
YOU COULD TRY!
--BUT YOU BEAT ME FAIRLY. I WOULD BE SHAMED.
SO I WILL SPEED YOU INSTEAD. THE GAMBLER SAID THAT THIS WAS WHAT YOU WANTED.
BUT I WILL SEE YOU AGAIN, JILL PRESTO. AT THE ENDING.
BECAUSE THERE WILL BE AN ENDING.
SOON.

"SO SOME OF YOU ARE UNHAPPY."
"SOME OF YOU THINK I'VE CHANGED..."
BUT I HAVE NOT CHANGED. I AM ONLY WHAT I EVER WAS.
MOTHER-- UNDERSTAND US--
ALWAYS WE HAVE BEEN ONE TRIBE. ONE FAMILY.
NOW WE FIGHT AND KILL EACH OTHER. IN THE NAME OF A CAUSE YOU HAVE YET TO EXPLAIN TO US.
WE HONOR YOU, BUT-- MANY OF US NEED A BETTER REASON TO FOLLOW.
THE REASON IS WHAT IT ALWAYS WAS, MISRAN.
THE WAR THAT HEAVEN WANTED. THAT HEAVEN STARTED.
DID THEY NOT DENY US THE GARDEN?
AND THEN THE CITY, EVEN THOUGH OUR HANDS RAISED IT?

OTHER NATIONS ARE BUILT ON A DREAM. OR AN ACCIDENT.
OURS-- ONLY OURS-- ON A GRIEVANCE.
FOR I AM RETURNED TO TELL YOU THAT YOU WAITING IS OVER. HEAVEN HANGS BY A THREAD.
AND WE ARE THE BLADE THAT WILL CUT THAT THREAD.
HAVE YOU NOT HATED HEAVEN FOR A THOUSAND, AND THEN A THOUSAND GENERATIONS OF MAN?
YOU KNOW WE HAVE.
GOOD, THEN.
WE CAN'T TOPPLE THE SILVER CITY.
NOT ALONE.
DID I SAY THAT WE WOULD BE ALONE?
IF THAT IS YOUR ONLY OBJECTION, MY SWEET SONS, MY PUISSANT DAUGHTERS--
--COME. AND BE SATISFIED.

THE CANYON DE CHELLY.

NORTHERN ARIZONA.

GET OUT OF MY WAY. I'VE ONLY GOT UNTIL-- THE SUN--
IT'S ALL RIGHT. THIS IS WHERE YOU WERE MEANT TO COME.
--UNTIL THE SUN--
OH JESUS.
I DIDN'T MAKE IT.
GRANDAD! HELP!
I'M COMING, I'M COMING.
DON'T LET HER FALL.
SHE THINKS SHE FAILED.
SHE DOESN'T KNOW WHERE SHE IS.
IT'S BEST SHE SLEEPS, IN ANY CASE.
BOIL THAT WATER UP, RACHEL.
HER REAL TRIAL IS STILL TO COME.

WHERE ARE WE GOING?
MOTHER SPOKE OF ALLIES. STRONG ONES, WHO'LL HELP US STRIKE AT HEAVEN.
MADNESS! WHAT ALLIES?

MY CHILDREN, I SAW A VISION A LONG TIME AGO.
I WAS IN THIS PLACE, AND A HOST DESCENDED TO MEET ME.

SO I SET ABOUT TO FORGE THIS HOST. ANGELS, BUT NOT OF HEAVEN.
I MET THEIR FATHER-- A SON OF HEAVEN-- IN THE SOFT PLACES. WE COUPLED THERE, AND I CONCEIVED.
NOT ONCE, BUT MANY TIMES.

AN ANGEL?
BUT ANGELS CANNOT--

THEY CANNOT, BUT I CAN. EVEN A BREATH MAKES MY WOMB QUICKEN.

THESE ARE YOUR BROTHERS AND YOUR SISTERS.
GIVE THEM *WELCOME.*

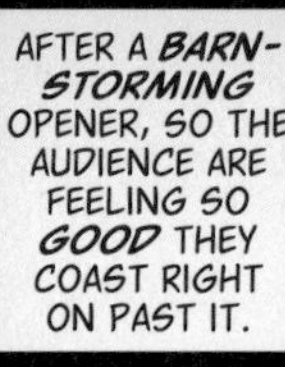

The BREACH
part 3 of 3

MIKE CAREY writer
PETER GROSS & RYAN KELLY artists
JARED K. FLETCHER lettering
DANIEL VOZZO colors
MICHAEL WM. KALUTA cover painter
MARIAH HUEHNER editor

Based on characters created by GAIMAN, KIETH & DRINGENBERG

WHOA THERE, HORSEY!
THAT'S AS FAR AS I GO ON A FIRST DATE.
AAA!
I WAS WASHING YOU CLEAN. FOR THE BLESSING.
MAYBE SO.
WHERE AM I?
IN MY GRANDAD'S HOGAN. PLEASE. THAT--THAT REALLY HURTS.
I WON'T TOUCH YOU AGAIN IF YOU DON'T WANT ME TO, JILL.
THE GUY WITH THE CIGAR-- HE SAID IF I MADE IT ACROSS THE DESERT, I'D FIND SOME PEOPLE WHO COULD HELP ME.
AND BLUE FLINT GIRL WARNED US THAT YOU'D BE COMING.
TOLD US WHAT YOU'D NEED.
STINKS OF SETUP.
DOESN'T IT?

AH, YOU ARE AWAKE. GOOD.
AND I GUESS YOU'D BE GRANDAD?
I AM HOSTEEN SAM BEGAI. YOU ARE WELCOME IN MY HOUSE.
YOU'VE BOILED THE WATER, RACHEL?
YES, GRANDAD. AND I SET THE SAND POTS OUT, TOO.
BLESS YOU. THEN I THINK THAT WE ARE READY.
HEY. READY FOR WHAT?
YOU WANT TO TALK TO ME INSTEAD OF AROUND ME?
READY FOR THE JOURNEY.
YOU'RE GOING SOMEWHERE?
NO. BUT YOU ARE. AND MY GRAND-DAUGHTER WILL GO WITH YOU.
HENCE THE PICNIC BASKET?
IT WILL BE NO PICNIC, JILL PRESTO.
YOU MUST TALK TO YOUR CHILD, BEFORE SHE IS BORN.
SHE LIES BREECH.
SHE INTENDS TO KILL YOU AS SHE COMES INTO THE WORLD.

LUCIFER'S CREATION.
THE ARMED CAMP OF THE LILIM.
MOTHER, WHAT ARE THEY? WHERE HAVE THEY COME FROM?
I TOLD YOU, MISRAN. THEY ARE YOUR BROTHERS AND YOUR SISTERS.
CONCEIVED AND BORN TO ME AND SANDALPHON IN THE SOFT PLACES OUTSIDE OF TIME.
BUT THAT CANNOT BE. IT IS A MIRACLE.
YES. IT IS MY MIRACLE.
THE QUICKENING POWER THAT LIVES IN ME AS FIRST WOMAN, OLDER THAN EVE.
LILITH.
SANDALPHON.
I HAVE MISSED YOU.
HAVE YOU? I HAVE ENDURED OUR PARTING VERY WELL.

WHAT WE HAVE DONE WAS NOT DONE FOR LOVE'S SAKE, BUT TO TOPPLE HEAVEN. YOU WANTED AN ARMY.
I HAVE GIVEN YOU TWO.
AND NOW IT BEGINS, MY DEAR ONES. NOW EONS OF INSULT WILL FINALLY BE AVENGED.
GOD AND HIS ANGELS WILL BLEED FOR WHAT THEY HAVE DONE TO US.
THIS IS YOUR MOTHER.
SHOW HER RESPECT.
WE MARCH ON THE SILVER CITY-- FROM THE PLAINS THAT STAND BELOW ITS EASTERN ASPECT.
I PRESUME YOU KNOW THE WAY.

SHE FACES THE *EAST.*

HEYA! SHE FACES THE *EAST.*

SHE FACES THE EAST AND SHE *EATS.*

RIGHT. ***WHAT*** DOES SHE EAT, EXACTLY?

IT'S LOPHOPHORA. ***PEYOTE.***

OH, FUCKING ***WONDERFUL.***

MY FETUS WANTS TO LAUNCH A *COMMANDO* RAID AGAINST ME FROM THE INSIDE.

YOU REALLY THINK GETTING *HIGH* IS AN ADEQUATE *RESPONSE?*

THERE IS NO *OTHER* WAY FOR YOU TO GO WHERE YOU *MUST* GO.

IT IS HARD TO PASS A *NEEDLE* THROUGH ITS OWN *EYE,* JILL PRESTO.

SHE CLOSES HER *EYES.*
HEYA! SHE CLOSES HER *EYES.*
SHE CLOSES HER *EYES* TO SEE THE ROAD.
AND IT *OPENS* BEFORE HER.

INTO THE EAST SHE *RISES* TO MEET IT.
OUT OF THE EAST IT RISES TO *MEET* HER.
TO PASS HER AND *RETURN.*

ALWAYS IT PASSES HER. ALWAYS IT *RETURNS.*
HEYA! SHE FACES THE *EAST.*

WHOA!
SHIT!
IT'S ALL RIGHT.
I-- I NEARLY FELL.
IT'S ALL RIGHT, JILL. I'VE GOT YOU.
FUCK! I'M FEELING A BIT DIZZY.
WERE WE SOMEWHERE ELSE JUST NOW?
MY GRANDFATHER'S HOUSE.
BUT NOW WE'VE FOUND THE ROAD.
OH YEAH. THE ROAD.
AND WE'VE GOT TO WALK IT.
RIGHT.
I THINK I HAD TOO MUCH TO DRINK OR SOMETHING.
I HOPE IT'S NOT TOO FAR.
NO. IT REALLY ISN'T.

"IN A WAY--"
"--WE'RE ALREADY *THERE.*"

THE SILVER CITY.
URIEL?
COUSIN?
ZONAQUEL. PLEASE. LEAVE ME BE.
I WILL NOT. THIS BROODING UNMANS YOU.
WE SIT IN COUNCIL, AND YOU ARE CALLED FOR. WILL YOU COME?
TO WHAT END?
TO DEBATE THE CRISIS. THE UNRAVELING OF THE WORLDS.
NOW THAT MICHAEL AND LUCIFER HAVE MISCARRIED, WE NEED A NEW PLAN.
A PLAN THAT WILL SUCCEED WHERE THE MORNINGSTAR AND MICHAEL HAVE FAILED?
I FEAR, COUSIN, THAT NOTHING IS LEFT NOW BUT TO MAKE OUR PEACE WITH DISSOLUTION.
BUT BY ALL MEANS LET US DEBATE IT, TOO.
IF NOTHING ELSE, IT PASSES THE TIME.

FUCK.
BE CAREFUL.
IF YOU WALK OFF THE PATH, YOU'LL NEVER FIND IT AGAIN.
LOOK AT THIS. I HAD THIS DOLL WHEN I WAS FIVE YEARS OLD.
HER NAME WAS MELANIE.
THIS PLACE ISN'T KANSAS, IS IT, RACHEL?
NO.
IT ISN'T EVEN NEW MEXICO. NOT ANY-MORE.
IT'S YOU, JILL. IT'S YOUR WOMB.
THAT'S WHY MY GRANDAD COULDN'T COME. HE'S NOT ALLOWED TO WALK THIS ROAD.

NEITHER ARE *YOU*, NAVAJO WITCH!
OW!
WHA--?
SHE DOESN'T *WANT* YOU HERE! *EITHER* OF YOU!
SHE'LL TEAR YOU INTO *PIECES* IF YOU GO ANY FURTHER!
LET *GO* OF ME!
MIND IF I *BORROW* THIS, HUGO?
NO! JILL, CA VA PAS, HEIN? CA VA *POINT!* YOU--
NICE *SEEING* YOU AGAIN, SCUMBAG.
ABRACA-FUCKING-DABRA.
VOOOOSH
YOU OKAY?
Y--YEAH. *THANK* YOU.
THEN LET'S KEEP *MOVING.* I THINK I *GET* THIS NOW.
THE TRICK IS, YOU BELIEVE IN *EVERYTHING* OR *NOTHING.*
IT WORKS *EITHER* WAY.

IT IS HARD TO THINK OF YOU AS MY BROTHER.
SAY HALF-BROTHER, RATHER. BUT THEN, THE LILIM ARE A RACE OF HALF-BROTHERS, FROM WHAT I HEAR.
MY NAME IS MAYEL.
HOW WILL WE KNOW WHEN WE HAVE REACHED OUR DESTINATION, MAYEL?
MOTHER SAYS THAT THERE WILL BE A SIGN. A GREAT LIGHT.
A GREAT LIGHT? AND WHAT WILL WE SEE BY IT?
ARMAGEDDON.
THE PLAIN THAT LIES UNDER HEAVEN IS CALLED ARMAGEDDON.
IT RESONATES THAT NAME, DOES IT NOT?

"I'M SURE ARMAGEDDON IS A PERFECT PLACE FOR NEW BEGINNINGS."
BE CAREFUL. AND BE POLITE.
YOU THINK THAT'S LIKELY TO HELP?
I DON'T KNOW. BUT I CAN FEEL FROM HERE HOW STRONG SHE IS.
HI. WHAT ARE YOU DOING?
I'M PLAYING.
YEAH? WELL IT'S MY SANDBOX.
LEAVE ME ALONE, MOTHER.
I DON'T WANT TO TALK TO YOU.
OH, YOU DON'T WANT TO TALK?
NO.
SO I SHOULD-- WHAT? TURN AROUND AND WALK BACK OUT OF HERE?
YES.

HEY, THIS IS ME. THIS IS MY BODY.
SEE THE ARROW? YOU ARE RIGHT-- FUCKING-- HERE!
SO YOU DO NOT GET TO TELL ME WHERE TO GO, OR WHAT TO SAY.
YOU WILL FUCKING WELL HEAR ME OUT!
OH, JEEZ.
YOU'RE LIKE-- SOME KIND OF EGG THAT GOT LAID INSIDE ME. LIKE FLIES LAY THEIR EGGS IN MEAT.
I JUST WANT YOU TO GET THE HELL OUT. THAT'S ALL I WANT.
I WILL! I WILL GO!
AND YOU'LL BE SORRY WHEN I DO.
BECAUSE YOU'LL DIE.
THAT'S ALL YOU KNOW HOW TO DO, ISN'T IT? RIP THINGS APART.
WELL FUCK YOU. FUCK HOWEVER MANY OF YOU THERE ARE.
JILL. HEY, JILL! THIS ISN'T HELPING.

I WAS RAPED BY A DECK OF CARDS. OU UNDERSTAND THAT? YOU'RE THE PRODUCT OF A RAPE.
AND IF I OULD HAVE GOTTEN O YOU WITH A BENT OATHANGER, YOU'D E DEAD. YOU'D BE FUCKING DEAD!
YOU SHOULD SHUT UP NOW. YOU'VE SAID ENOUGH.
I'M TELLING THE TRUTH!
YOU'RE COMMITTING SUICIDE.
LITTLE GIRL--
NOEMA.
NOEMA. I THINK YOU AND YOUR MOM GOT OFF TO A BAD--
LEAVE ME ALONE.
YEAH, WELL I WILL. BUT I WANT YOU TO TALK TO EACH OTHER FIRST.
I WANT YOU TO EXPLAIN WHAT IT IS YOU'RE SCARED OF.
I'M NOT SCARED.
YES YOU ARE. YOU THINK I HAVEN'T SEEN SCARED BEFORE?
YOU'RE ALMOST PEEING YOURSELF.
SHE WANTS TO KILL ME. SHE SAID IT.
SHE WANTS TO KILL ME LIKE SHE KILLED MY BROTHER.

WHAT?
HER BROTHER?
WHAT DID YOU SAY?
YES! MY BROTHER EIKON!
YOUR BROTHER TRIED TO BRAINWASH ME. HE TRIED TO MAKE ME LOVE HIM.
WHAT I DID TO HIM WAS PURE SELF-DEFENSE.
WHY DID HE HAVE TO MAKE YOU?
HE WAS YOURS. YOU SHOULD HAVE LOVED HIM BECAUSE HE WAS YOURS.
IT-- IT DIDN'T FEEL THAT WAY.
YOU DON'T UNDERSTAND WHAT IT WAS LIKE. WITH THE BASANOS I WAS HELPLESS.
THEY TORTURED ME. THEY DID THIS TO ME.
THEY MADE ME INTO A-- A TOY.
I KILLED EIKON BECAUSE I COULDN'T THINK OF ANY OTHER WAY TO GET FREE.
SKIP IT. I DIDN'T COME HERE TO BEG. COME ON, RACHEL, MAKE WITH THE RUBY SLIPPERS.

IF I LET YOU BE FREE--
--DO YOU THINK YOU'D LOVE ME?
WHAT?
IF I LET YOU BE FREE--
NO, I HEARD YOU. I JUST DIDN'T BELIEVE IT.
TRUTH? RIGHT NOW I FIND YOU ABOUT AS LOVABLE AS A TAPEWORM.
BUT-- HOW CAN I KNOW? HOW CAN I ANSWER THAT?
NOEMA, IS THERE A WAY FOR YOU TO BE BORN THAT DOESN'T KILL JILL?
THEN MAYBE THE TWO OF YOU COULD HANG LOOSE AND SEE WHAT DEVELOPS.
IF I SET MY POWER ASIDE-- JUST AS I WAS COMING OUT-- I COULD BE LIKE ANY BABY COMING OUT.
BUT THEN IF YOU WANTED TO HURT ME-- THERE'D BE A FEW SECONDS WHEN YOU'D BE ABLE TO.

WILL YOU PROMISE NOT TO HURT HER, NOEMA?
WHAT KIND OF A QUESTION IS THAT?
WHAT WOULD IT EVEN MEAN IF I SAID THAT? IT'S JUST WORDS.
WELL, THE ONLY WAY THIS IS GOING TO WORK IS IF YOU TWO DECIDE TO TRUST EACH OTHER.
WILL YOU PROMISE?
YEAH. OKAY. I-- I PROMISE. IF YOU LET ME LIVE, I WON'T HURT YOU.
HURTING YOU WASN'T THE POINT.
HEY, THIS IS GOING TO SOUND STUPID, BUT-- IF YOU LIKE DOLLS--
--THIS ONE'S CALLED MEL.
THANK YOU, MOTHER. I'LL THINK ABOUT WHAT WE'VE SAID.
BUT I NEED TO BE BORN NOW--
--SO YOU SHOULD PROBABLY WAKE UP.

NUUUUH!
WHAT HAPPENED, RACHEL? WHAT PASSED BETWEEN THEM?
GRANDAD! WELL, THEY-- THEY TALKED, AND--
OH JESUS.
ARE YOU OKAY, JILL?
NO, I'M IN FUCKING AGONY. GUUUUH!
I THINK SHE'S COMING.
AND I THINK THE--
...
--THE TRUCE IS OVER. OH GOD!
GRANDAD, WHAT SHALL WE DO?
HOLD HER HAND, RACHEL. I HAVE TO SEE IF THE BABY HAS TURNED.
HOWEVER IT GOES, THIS WILL BE QUICK NOW.

THERE. THAT IS THE LIGHT I PROMISED YOU.
AND THIS IS OUR HOUR. THE TIME FORETOLD.

"ALL THINGS COME TOGETHER.
"ALL THINGS ARE POISED, AS WAS INTENDED.
"AND NOW WE PUSH."
The End

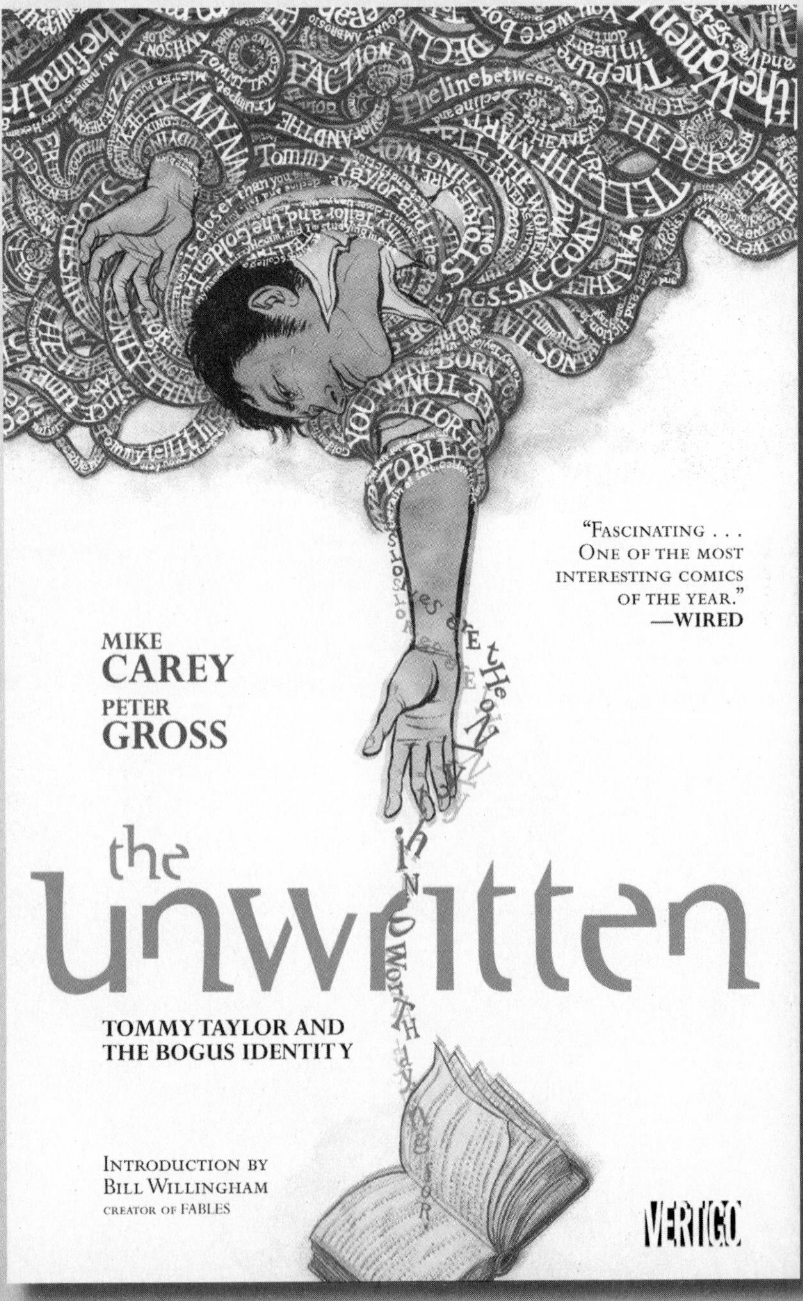